Streamlines: Selected Readings on Single Topics

The Natural World

Marjorie Ford
Stanford University

Jon Ford
College of Alameda

Houghton Mifflin Company

Boston   New York

SENIOR SPONSORING EDITOR: Suzanne Phelps Weir
SENIOR ASSOCIATE EDITOR: Janet Edmonds
EDITORIAL ASSISTANT: Tamara Jachimowicz
EDITORIAL PRODUCTION COORDINATOR: Carla Thompson
PRODUCTION/DESIGN COORDINATOR: Jennifer Meyer Dare
SENIOR MANUFACTURING COORDINATOR: Priscilla J. Abreu
SENIOR MARKETING MANAGER: Nancy Lyman

COVER DESIGN: Rebecca Fagan
COVER IMAGE: Jim Wehtje/PhotoDisc

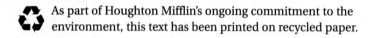 As part of Houghton Mifflin's ongoing commitment to the environment, this text has been printed on recycled paper.

Acknowledgments appear on pp. 115–116, which constitute an extension of the copyright page.

Printed in the U.S.A.

Library of Congress Catalog Card Number: 98-72029
ISBN: 0-395-86802-5

23456789–CS–02 01 00 99

CONTENTS

A series of four books on intriguing, relevant topics, *Streamlines: Selected Readings on Single Topics* are an innovation among composition textbooks for college writing courses. Designed to encourage creativity, critical thinking, and research in writing classrooms, the series presents a range of texts to choose from: classic and contemporary essays, literature, journalistic writing, research-based writing, and student essays. The books can be used individually or in combination. Each book allows instructors to delve deeply into single topics—Learning, Health, the Natural World, and Mass Culture and Electronic Media—while allowing for a variety of teaching approaches. Some instructors may assign one or two of the books in addition to readings in a general purpose reader and a rhetoric/handbook to provide strong thematic focus for the course. Other instructors may feel comfortable setting aside three or four weeks toward the end of a semester to investigate a single issue, perhaps with a goal of a final project such as a longer oral or written assignment. Yet other instructors may structure their course around several of the books, perhaps making cross-references between related texts in different volumes of the series.

Format

Streamlines' major strengths include accessibility and ease of use, which stem in part from their consistent format. Each book is approximately 130 pages long, includes 13 to 16 readings, and contains a substantial, but not overwhelming, apparatus—a brief introduction, five study and discussion questions, and two suggestions for writing projects for each reading selection. Several topics for thought, research, and writing at the end of each book help students synthesize the individual selections. The books introduce students to the subject matter of the volume with an initial poem. Every book is divided into four sections, which contain several thematically related works.

The Individual Readers

Learning   This volume contains readings that address fundamental questions that philosophers, educators, and psychologists ask about how and why people learn, and examine events and attitudes that can make learning difficult as well as pleasurable. The issue of learning (both in and out of the classroom) is especially relevant for first-year composition students to examine in depth. The first section of the reader, "Learning from Experience," explores the learning that results from the revelations that arise from learning experiences. "Learning at School," the next section, focuses on classrooms and explores different aspects of them. "Learning and Diversity" considers ways that language, cultural, and class differences become issues in education, while the final section, "Thinking About How We Learn," looks at how intelligence is defined and how effective education programs can help to build strong communities.

Health   Students are concerned about many health issues, and we have tried to confront some of these concerns in this volume. The selections engage interest by closely viewing health concerns that are foremost in students' minds. The first section, "Doctors," examines how both caring, supportive relations with physicians and self-awareness figure into recovery processes. "Self-Image and High-Risk Behavior" discusses relationships among self-esteem, body image, and wellness, while the third section, "Mental Health," examines relationships between psychological stress and physical illness as well as some of the symptoms, causes, and consequences of mental disorders such as depression and manic depression. The final section, "Healing and Community," provides a broader perspective on ways that doctors and patients can work together to create caring communities dedicated to good health.

The Natural World   Nature inspires people of all ages; it is also an area for controversies and concerns about the use and preservation of species and ecosystems. This volume begins with an exploration of "The Experience of Nature," which includes inspirational narratives of travels in nature. The second section, "Nature and the Scientific Mind," explores the ways scientists perceive nature and theorize about natural processes. "Environmental Issues: Protection and Preservation" presents students with controversies surrounding pollution, environmental disasters, and the movement to protect the earth and its species. Finally, in "Nature and the Philosophical Imagination," students are introduced to meditative essays that reflect on philosophical and spiritual meanings that can be found through contact with nature.

Mass Culture and Electronic Media   At the heart of many students' cultural experiences are the electronic media—particularly radio, television, CDs, and the Internet. We begin this volume with "Cult Heroes and Icons," which presents readings that bridge discussions of the older heroes of the mass media of cartoons and comic books with heroes of the newer media. The second section, "Family, Gender, and the Electronic Media," provides analysis of the impact of the electronic media on women and family life. "Ethnicity and Electronic Media" reflects on media images of minority groups. Finally, in "Reality Re-configured: Reading the New Electronic Media," media theorists and researchers discuss how television and the Internet influence our perceptions of reality and suggest ways to "read" the media insightfully in order to accurately discern underlying messages.

We would like to thank Alison Zetterquist and Janet Edmonds at Houghton Mifflin, and our student writers. For helping us refine our ideas, we would also like to thank our reviewers:

James K. Bell, College of San Mateo
Donald Blount, University of South Carolina—Aiken
Keith Coplin, Colby Community College
Jan Delasara, Metropolitan State College of Denver
Patrick Dolan, Arapahoe Community College
Frank Fennell, Loyola University
Judith Funston, State University of New York at Potsdam
Sara McLaughlin, Texas Tech University
Denish Martone, New York University
Lawrence E. Musgrove, University of Southern Indiana
Julie Nichols, Okaloosa-Walton Community College
Pearlie M. Peters, Rider University
Katherine Ploeger, Modesto Junior College, California State
    University, Stanislaus
John Reilly, Loyola Marymount University
Patricia Roberts, Rivier College
Kristen Snoddy, Indiana University, Kokomo
Jan Strever, Gonzaga University

M. F.
J. F.

Nature always wears the colors of the spirit.

RALPH WALDO EMERSON

Genius is a light which makes the darkness visible, like the lightning's flash, which perchance shatters the temple of knowledge itself.

HENRY DAVID THOREAU

Only within the moment of time represented by the present century has one species—man—acquired significant power to alter the nature of his world. **RACHEL CARSON**

Nature has always had the power to nourish, heal, and inspire. Many naturalists believe that nature is our greatest teacher, wise yet mysterious, beautiful, wild, and dangerous. A remarkable sunset, an isolated beach at dawn, an earthquake, or a hurricane may remind us that the world is extraordinary and that nature has the power to feed or destroy. Nature embodies the principle that the best way to learn is from an experience that has constancy yet is forever changing. We will be wise to pay attention: to learn to hear, to see, to try to understand nature's messages. If we value nature's beauty and power, we must work to respect and preserve the natural world that we have inherited.

Most of us live in communities that are largely defined by laws and technology. Intent on getting through our daily routines and on maintaining a comfortable lifestyle, we often allow ourselves to become prisoners of deadlines, traffic jams, subways, pollution, skyscrapers, computer chips, and polyester. We often forget about how much the natural world has to provide—adventure, beauty, perspective, and peace. We have developed this anthology to help you think more deeply about the fundamental but not always apparent role that the natural world plays in all of our lives. Becoming more conscious of the patterns, rhythms, and mysterious qualities of nature, as well as of the risks of upsetting the natural world's balance, can help you to improve the quality of your own life and the quality of life in your community.

Each section of this anthology looks at the natural world from a unique perspective. We begin with "The Experience of Nature." The essays in this section tell of intense and miraculous experiences in the natural world. The next group of essays, "Nature and the Scientific Mind," focuses on the different ways that scientists are attempting to better understand nature and human nature. The essays in the third section, "Environmental Issues: Protection and Preservation," present concrete examples and persuasive warnings of the consequences of exploiting the earth or any of its inhabitants. The final section of this anthology, "Nature and the Philosophical Imagination," offers some of the major philosophical essays that explore ways that the mind and spirit are connected to nature.

We hope that reading these selections will help you to realize how the writers' experiences in nature have challenged and deepened their human capabilities. We also hope that these selections will inspire you to belong more fully to the natural world.

The Experience of Nature

The selections in this section capture revelatory experiences in nature. By reading and reflecting on them, we can begin to see how a better knowledge of the natural world can help us to develop perspective on our daily routines, expectations, and goals. In "The Khumbu Icefall," from the recent national best-seller *Into Thin Air,* Jon Krakauer explains the practical challenges of climbing the most demanding and terrifying icefall on the route to Mount Everest. He concludes with the spiritual value of his climb: "As dawn washed the darkness from the sky, the shattered glacier was revealed to be a three-dimensional landscape of phantasmal beauty." In "The Solace of Open Spaces," Gretel Ehrlich examines the effect that Wyoming's open space has had on her, showing us how the vast open spaces have helped her to find new perspective: "Space has a spiritual equivalent and can heal what is divided and burdensome in us." In both selections, landscapes and vistas provide the beauty and peace that help to quiet fears.

The next selection reflects on how the landscape can help us to understand history, art, and culture. In "The Stone Horse," Barry Lopez travels through a remote area of the southwestern desert to face a wild animal, a stone horse, made three hundred years ago by the Quechan people. As Lopez imagines what the lives of these people and their ancestors were like, he marvels at the artistic quality of the horse carved into the stone pavement and gains perspective: "I remembered that history . . . ran deeper than Mexico, deeper than the Spanish, was a kind of medicine. It permitted the great breadth of human expression to reverberate, and it did not urge you to locate its apotheosis in the present."

The final selection in this section, Annie Dillard's "Total Eclipse," tells of an awakening, a type of rebirth. After being a witness to the coming of darkness, a total eclipse created when the moon covered the sun, Dillard sees new meanings in the sunlight and in being alive: "As adults we are almost all adept at waking up. We have so mastered the transition we have forgotten we ever learned it." The earth's darkness during the eclipse had begun to obliterate Dillard's sense of self, which with the new, renewed light she values more.

Nature and the Scientific Mind

Many of the most profound scientific inquiries involve an attempt to find a unified theory of nature. In the first selection, "Evolution as Fact and Theory," Stephen Jay Gould argues that evolution is one of the most important scientific theories of all time because it encourages us to think deeply about the origins of life itself. Gould believes, despite attacks by modern creationists, that a scientific attempt to understand nature will help individuals to know themselves better. Although scientific theory can lead to deeper understanding, Farley Mowat, in "Learning to See," shares what he has learned while applying his scientific knowledge and equipment to study misperceptions of the wolf population by scientists as well as ranchers and hunters. He seeks "to know the wolves, not for what they were supposed to be but for what they actually were." His scientific study of the Arctic wolves becomes a process of self-education. He concludes that learning to be more open-minded is a way of finding spiritual healing. More critical of scientific theory and progress, the next essay, by Terry Tempest Williams, "The Clan of One-Breasted Women," shows how scientific knowledge can also lead to betrayal. Williams has reason to believe that the fallout from nuclear testing in the Utah desert may have caused the death of her mother and grandmother from breast cancer. Tempest Williams uses words as her weapons, writing about her participation in a protest against continued scientific testing of nuclear weapons in the desert near her home.

The essays in this section help us to see that science can be a powerful tool for understanding nature and learning about ourselves; at the same time, they warn us to think about the consequences of putting too much faith in science's ability to harness and control the natural world for our own ends.

Environmental Issues: Protection and Preservation

All of the essays in this section discuss the dangerous consequences of exploiting the earth and its species, reminding us that future generations are unlikely to condone our lack of prudent concern for the integrity of the natural world that supports life. In "Thinking Like a

Mountain," Aldo Leopold personifies the mountains' wisdom and their understanding that the wildness of plant and animal communities have developed their own preservation cycle. Rachel Carson, in "The Obligation to Endure," makes a forceful argument against scientific knowledge that is applied with insufficient understanding of possible consequences: "The public must decide whether it wishes to continue on the present road, and it can do so only when in full possession of the facts." Carson specifically alerts us to the potentially dangerous consequences of controlling insect populations with chemicals whose long-term impact we cannot accurately predict.

The next two selections focus on the endangered species of mountain gorillas in the Virunga Mountains of Africa. In the first selection, "Decimation by Poachers," Dian Fossey writes about her sadness and outrage upon learning about the death of one of the gorillas that she had been protecting and studying for over ten years. The poachers were concerned only with their own immediate and short-term material gains. Fossey seeks to make people think about the blatant disregard of an endangered species. In the next essay, student writer Lindsey Munro explores Fossey's legacy. An idealistic researcher, Munro nevertheless wants to develop a practical and realistic perspective on how to approach problems related to endangered species.

Nature and the Philosophical Imagination

The meditative essays selected for this section examine ways that philosophical and spiritual meanings can be found through contact with nature. In "Nature," Ralph Waldo Emerson, whose transcendentalism has had a strong influence on the modern environmental movement, asks people to think more deeply about the relationships between nature and the soul. Emerson defines the sensibility of the lover of nature as one that is balanced and open to his or her childlike self: "He is one whose inward and outward sense are still truly adjusted to each other; who has retained the spirit of infancy even into the era of manhood." The next selection, from Henry David Thoreau's "Walking," provides provocative examples to support a central claim that continues to influence naturalists and environmentalists: "In Wildness is the preservation of the world. . . . Life consists with wildness. The most alive is the wildest." The next essay, "The Etiquette of Freedom," by poet and environmentalist Gary Snyder, develops Thoreau's concept: "To be truly free one must take on the basic conditions as they are—painful, impermanent, open, imperfect—and then be grateful for impermanence and the freedom it grants us. . . . Wildness is not just the 'preservation of the world'—it *is* the world."

The final selections offer visionary perspectives on how one might understand and experience the natural world. In "She Unnames

Them," Ursula K. Le Guin's narrator imagines a revised version of the biblical creation myth of Adam and Eve. The story opens with the narrator's unnaming all of the animals, releasing them from their imprisonment in human labels. Then she leaves Adam alone in the garden as she steps out into the new world, where she will have the opportunity to create a new language, another naming system, one that will allow her to reflect a fresh vision of the natural world. In "Sea Change," Kathleen Norris presents another vision of the meaning of time and space and the spirit through her descriptions of and reflections on the Great Plains: "It's a dangerous place, this vast ocean of prairie. Something happens to us here."

All of us belong to nature. We have much to be thankful for—many landscapes and environments, many plants and animals, that deserve our respect. In the pages that follow, the authors help us to see, hear, and understand the majesty and the wonders that can be ours.

Emplumada

LORNA DEE CERVANTES

When summer ended
the leaves of snapdragons withered
taking their shrill-colored mouths with them.
They were still, so quiet. They were
violet where umber now is. She hated   5
and she hated to see
them go. Flowers

born when the weather was good—this
she thinks of, watching the branch of peaches
daring their ways above the fence, and further,   10
two hummingbirds, hovering, stuck to each other,
arcing their bodies in grim determination
to find what is good, what is
given them to find. These are warriors

distancing themselves from history.   15
They find peace
in the way they contain the wind
and are gone.

The Experience of Nature

The Khumbu Icefall

JON KRAKAUER

Jon Krakauer (b. 1954) was raised in Corvalis, Oregon, and traces his obsession with mountain climbing to his first climbing experiences when he was only eight years old. After graduating from college in 1975, Krakauer worked as an itinerant carpenter to make money to support his expeditions. In 1981 he began his career as a journalist, writing about what he loves most. A collection of his essays was published in Eiger Dreams *(1992). His second book,* Into the Wild *(1996), is the story of a young adventurer who gets lost in the vast Alaska territory. His third book, the best-selling* Into Thin Air *(1997), began as an assignment for* Outside *magazine. Krakauer joined a commercial expedition to Mount Everest led by Rob Hall, one of the world's most respected guides. When members of Hall's expedition and another led by Scott Fischer got caught in a storm on the summit, two clients and three guides (including Hall and Fischer) perished. In the selection that follows, Krakauer captures one of the most dramatic episodes in the days leading up to the deadly summit attempt, while showing how commercialization and high-tech equipment have affected the challenges of mountain climbing.*

Our route to the summit would follow the Khumbu Glacier up the   1
lower half of the mountain. From the *bergschrund** at 23,000 feet that
marked its upper end, this great river of ice flowed two and a half
miles down a relatively gentle valley called the Western Cwm. As the
glacier inched over humps and dips in the Cwm's underlying strata, it
fractured into countless vertical fissures—crevasses. Some of these
crevasses were narrow enough to step across; others were eighty feet
wide, several hundred feet deep, and ran half a mile from end to end.
The big ones were apt to be vexing obstacles to our ascent, and when
hidden beneath a crust of snow they would pose a serious hazard, but
the challenges presented by the crevasses in the Cwm had proven
over the years to be predictable and manageable.

The Icefall was a different story. No part of the South Col route was   2
feared more by climbers. At around 20,000 feet, where the glacier
emerged from the lower end of the Cwm, it pitched abruptly over a
precipitous drop. This was the infamous Khumbu Icefall, the most
technically demanding section on the entire route.

---

*A *bergschrund* is a deep slit that delineates a glacier's upper terminus; it forms as the
body of ice slides away from the steeper wall immediately above, leaving a gap between
glacier and rock.

The movement of the glacier in the Icefall has been measured at   3
between three and four feet a day. As it skids down the steep, irregular
terrain in fits and starts, the mass of ice splinters into a jumble of
huge, tottering blocks called *seracs,* some as large as office buildings.
Because the climbing route wove under, around, and between hundreds of these unstable towers, each trip through the Icefall was a little
like playing a round of Russian roulette: sooner or later any given
serac was going to fall over without warning, and you could only hope
you weren't beneath it when it toppled. Since 1963, when . . . Jake
Breitenbach was crushed by an avalanching serac to become the Icefall's first victim, eighteen other climbers had died here.

The previous winter, as he had done in winters past, Hall had   4
consulted with the leaders of all the expeditions planning to climb
Everest in the spring, and together they'd agreed on one team among
them who would be responsible for establishing and maintaining a
route through the Icefall. For its trouble, the designated team was to
be paid $2,200 from each of the other expeditions on the mountain. In
recent years this cooperative approach had been met with wide, if not
universal, acceptance, but it wasn't always so.

The first time one expedition thought to charge another to travel   5
through the ice was in 1988, when a lavishly funded American team
announced that any expedition that intended to follow the route
they'd engineered up the Icefall would have to fork over $2,000. Some
of the other teams on the mountain that year, failing to understand
that Everest was no longer merely a mountain but a commodity as
well, were incensed. And the greatest hue and cry came from Rob
Hall, who was leading a small, impecunious New Zealand team.

Hall carped that the Americans were "violating the spirit of the hills"   6
and practicing a shameful form of alpine extortion, but Jim Frush, the
unsentimental attorney who was the leader of the American group,
remained unmoved. Hall eventually agreed through clenched teeth to
send Frush a check and was granted passage through the Icefall.
(Frush later reported that Hall never made good on his IOU.)

Within two years, however, Hall did an about-face and came to see   7
the logic of treating the Icefall as a toll road. Indeed, from 1993 through
'95 he volunteered to put in the route and collect the toll himself. In the
spring of 1996 he elected not to assume responsibility for the Icefall,
but he was happy to pay the leader of a rival commercial* expedition—
a Scottish Everest veteran named Mal Duff—to take over the job. Long

---

*Although I use "commercial" to denote any expedition organized as a money-making
venture, not all commercial expeditions are guided. For instance, Mal Duff—who
charged his clients considerably less than the $65,000 fee requested by Hall and Fischer—
provided leadership and the essential infrastructure necessary to climb Everest (food,
tents, bottled oxygen, fixed ropes, Sherpa support staff, and so on) but did not purport to
act as a guide; the climbers on his team were assumed to be sufficiently skilled to get
themselves safely up Everest and back down again.

before we'd even arrived at Base Camp, a team of Sherpas employed by Duff had blazed a zigzag path through the seracs, stringing out more than a mile of rope and installing some sixty aluminum ladders over the broken surface of the glacier. The ladders belonged to an enterprising Sherpa from the village of Gorak Shep who turned a nice profit by renting them out each season.

So it came to pass that at 4:45 A.M. on Saturday, April 13, I found   8
myself at the foot of the fabled Icefall, strapping on my crampons in the frigid predawn gloom.

Crusty old alpinists who've survived a lifetime of close scrapes like   9
to counsel young protégés that staying alive hinges on listening carefully to one's "inner voice." Tales abound of one or another climber who decided to remain in his or her sleeping bag after detecting some inauspicious vibe in the ether and thereby survived a catastrophe that wiped out others who failed to heed the portents.

I didn't doubt the potential value of paying attention to subcon-   10
scious cues. As I waited for Rob to lead the way, the ice underfoot emitted a series of loud cracking noises, like small trees being snapped in two, and I felt myself wince with each pop and rumble from the glacier's shifting depths. Problem was, my inner voice resembled Chicken Little: it was screaming that I was about to die, but it did that almost every time I laced up my climbing boots. I therefore did my damnedest to ignore my histrionic imagination and grimly followed Rob into the eerie blue labyrinth.

Although I'd never been in an icefall as frightening as the Khumbu,   11
I'd climbed many other icefalls. They typically have vertical or even overhanging passages that demand considerable expertise with ice ax and crampons. There was certainly no lack of steep ice in the Khumbu Icefall, but all of it had been rigged with ladders or ropes or both, rendering the conventional tools and techniques of ice climbing largely superfluous.

I soon learned that on Everest not even the rope—the quintessen-   12
tial climber's accoutrement—was to be utilized in the time-honored manner. Ordinarily, one climber is tied to one or two partners with a 150-foot length of rope, making each person directly responsible for the life of the others; roping up in this fashion is a serious and very intimate act. In the Icefall, though, expediency dictated that each of us climb independently, without being physically connected to one another in any way.

Mal Duff's Sherpas had anchored a static line of rope that extended   13
from the bottom of the Icefall to its top. Attached to my waist was a three-foot-long safety tether with a carabiner, or snap-link, at the distal end. Security was achieved not by roping myself to a teammate but rather by clipping my safety tether to the fixed line and sliding it up the rope as I ascended. Climbing in this fashion, we would be able to move as quickly as possible through the most dangerous parts of the

Icefall, and we wouldn't have to entrust our lives to teammates whose skill and experience were unknown. As it turned out, not once during the entire expedition would I ever have reason to rope myself to another climber.

If the Icefall required few orthodox climbing techniques, it demanded a whole new repertoire of skills in their stead—for instance, the ability to tiptoe in mountaineering boots and crampons across three wobbly ladders lashed end to end, bridging a sphincter-clenching chasm. There were many such crossings, and I never got used to them. 14

At one point I was balanced on an unsteady ladder in the predawn gloaming, stepping tenuously from one bent rung to the next, when the ice supporting the ladder on either end began to quiver as if an earthquake had struck. A moment later came an explosive roar as a large serac somewhere close above came crashing down. I froze, my heart in my throat, but the avalanching ice passed fifty yards to the left, out of sight, without doing any damage. After waiting a few minutes to regain my composure I resumed my herky-jerky passage to the far side of the ladder. 15

The glacier's continual and often violent state of flux added an element of uncertainty to every ladder crossing. As the glacier moved, crevasses would sometimes compress, buckling ladders like toothpicks; other times a crevasse might expand, leaving a ladder dangling in the air, only tenuously supported, with neither end mounted on solid ice. Anchors* securing the ladders and lines routinely melted out when the afternoon sun warmed the surrounding ice and snow. Despite daily maintenance, there was a very real danger that any given rope might pull loose under body weight. 16

But if the Icefall was strenuous and terrifying, it had a surprising allure as well. As dawn washed the darkness from the sky, the shattered glacier was revealed to be a three-dimensional landscape of phantasmal beauty. The temperature was six degrees Fahrenheit. My crampons crunched reassuringly into the glacier's rind. Following the fixed line, I meandered through a vertical maze of crystalline blue stalagmites. Sheer rock buttresses seamed with ice pressed in from both edges of the glacier, rising like the shoulders of a malevolent god. Absorbed by my surroundings and the gravity of the labor, I lost myself in the unfettered pleasures of ascent, and for an hour or two actually forgot to be afraid. 17

Three-quarters of the way to Camp One, Hall remarked at a rest stop that the Icefall was in better shape than he'd ever seen it: "The route's a bloody freeway this season." But only slightly higher, at 19,000 feet, the ropes brought us to the base of a gargantuan, perilously balanced serac. As massive as a twelve-story building, it loomed over 18

---

*Three-foot long aluminum stakes called pickets were used to anchor ropes and ladders to snow slopes; when the terrain was hard glacial ice, "ice screws" were employed: hollow, threaded tubes about ten inches long that were twisted into the frozen glacier.

our heads, leaning 30 degrees past vertical. The route followed a natural catwalk that angled sharply up the overhanging face: we would
have to climb up and over the entire off-kilter tower to escape its
threatening tonnage.

Safety, I understood, hinged on speed. I huffed toward the relative   19
security of the serac's crest with all the haste I could muster, but since
I wasn't acclimatized my fastest pace was no better than a crawl. Every
four or five steps I'd have to stop, lean against the rope, and suck desperately at the thin, bitter air, searing my lungs in the process.

I reached the top of the serac without it collapsing and flopped   20
breathless onto its flat summit, my heart pounding like a jackhammer.
A little later, around 8:30 A.M., I arrived at the top of the Icefall itself,
just beyond the last of the seracs. The safety of Camp One didn't supply much peace of mind, however: I couldn't stop thinking about the
ominously tilted slab a short distance below, and the fact that I would
have to pass beneath its faltering bulk at least seven more times if I was
going to make it to the summit of Everest. Climbers who snidely deni-
grate this as the Yak Route, I decided, had obviously never been
through the Khumbu Icefall.

QUESTIONS FOR DISCUSSION

1 What factors make climbing the Khumbu Icefall the most demanding challenge on the route to the summit of Mount Everest?
   Why have nineteen climbers died on this icefall?

2 Why has the icefall been made into a toll road? What is your opinion about this decision?

3 Why does Krakauer think about the alpine climbers who listen to
   their inner voices, or subconscious, before embarking on a dangerous journey? How does Krakauer handle his fear?

4 Why do you think Krakauer finds this frightening and challenging climb alluring? What impact does his journey have on his
   mind and spirit? What do you think of his decision to climb
   Mount Everest?

5 What have you learned about mountain climbing and the power
   of nature from reading this selection?

IDEAS FOR WRITING

1 Can you imagine yourself climbing the Khumbu Icefall? Write a
   paper that explores what you think you might do, as well as how
   you think you would feel and react.

2 Write a research essay on the life of a famous climber or adventurer and his or her belief in the power of nature.

The Solace of Open Spaces

GRETEL EHRLICH

Gretel Ehrlich (b. 1946) was raised in California. She attended Bennington College, film school at the University of California at Los Angeles, and the New School for Social Research in New York. In 1976, she settled permanently in Wyoming after doing a documentary on sheep herders there and began writing about this experience. The selection that follows is from the first chapter of The Solace of Open Spaces *(1985). She worked for five years on this book in order to capture the intensity of the Wyoming landscape and way of life. Ehrlich has said about her vision as a writer, "The truest art I would strive for in any work would be to give the page the same qualities as earth: weather would land on it harshly; light would elucidate the most difficult truths; wind would sweep away obtuse padding." Ehrlich has also written a book of fiction,* Heart Mountain *(1988), the nonfiction essay collection* Islands, the Universe, Home *(1991), and* A Match to the Heart: One Woman's Story of Being Struck by Lightning *(1994). All of her writing explores the relationship between the natural and spiritual worlds.*

1   It's May and I've just awakened from a nap, curled against sagebrush the way my dog taught me to sleep—sheltered from wind. A front is pulling the huge sky over me, and from the dark a hailstone has hit me on the head. I'm trailing a band of two thousand sheep across a stretch of Wyoming badlands, a fifty-mile trip that takes five days because sheep shade up in hot sun and won't budge until it's cool. Bunched together now, and excited into a run by the storm, they drift across dry land, tumbling into draws like water and surging out again onto the rugged, choppy plateaus that are the building blocks of this state.

2   The name Wyoming comes from an Indian word meaning "at the great plains," but the plains are really valleys, great arid valleys, sixteen hundred square miles, with the horizon bending up on all sides into mountain ranges. This gives the vastness a sheltering look.

3   Winter lasts six months here. Prevailing winds spill snowdrifts to the east, and new storms from the northwest replenish them. This white bulk is sometimes dizzying, even nauseating, to look at. At twenty, thirty, and forty degrees below zero, not only does your car not work, but neither do your mind and body. The landscape hardens into a dungeon of space. During the winter, while I was riding to find a new calf, my jeans froze to the saddle, and in the silence that such cold creates I felt like the first person on earth, or the last.

4   Today the sun is out—only a few clouds billowing. In the east, where the sheep have started off without me, the benchland tilts up in

a series of eroded red-earthed mesas, planed flat on top by a million years of water; behind them, a bold line of muscular scarps rears up ten thousand feet to become the Big Horn Mountains. A tidal pattern is engraved into the ground, as if left by the sea that once covered this state. Canyons curve down like galaxies to meet the oncoming rush of flat land.

To live and work in this kind of open country, with its hundred-mile   5
views, is to lose the distinction between background and foreground. When I asked an older ranch hand to describe Wyoming's openness, he said, "It's all a bunch of nothing—wind and rattlesnakes—and so much of it you can't tell where you're going or where you've been and it don't make much difference." John, a sheepman I know, is tall and handsome and has an explosive temperament. He has a perfect intuition about people and sheep. They call him "Highpockets," because he's so long-legged; his graceful stride matches the distances he has to cover. He says, "Open space hasn't affected me at all. It's all the people moving in on it." The huge ranch he was born on takes up much of one county and spreads into another state; to put 100,000 miles on his pickup in three years and never leave home is not unusual. A friend of mine has an aunt who ranched on Powder River and didn't go off her place for eleven years. When her husband died, she quickly moved to town, bought a car, and drove around the States to see what she'd been missing.

Most people tell me they've simply driven through Wyoming, as if   6
there were nothing to stop for. Or else they've skied in Jackson Hole, a place Wyomingites acknowledge uncomfortably because its green beauty and chic affluence are mismatched with the rest of the state. Most of Wyoming has a "lean-to" look. Instead of big, roomy barns and Victorian houses, there are dugouts, low sheds, log cabins, sheep camps, and fence lines that look like driftwood blown haphazardly into place. People here still feel pride because they live in such a harsh place, part of the glamorous cowboy past, and they are determined not to be the victims of a mining-dominated future.

Most characteristic of the state's landscape is what a developer   7
euphemistically describes as "indigenous growth right up to your front door"—a reference to waterless stands of salt sage, snakes, jack rabbits, deerflies, red dust, a brief respite of wildflowers, dry washes, and no trees. In the Great Plains the vistas look like music, like Kyries of grass, but Wyoming seems to be the doing of a mad architect— tumbled and twisted, ribboned with faded, deathbed colors, thrust up and pulled down as if the place had been startled out of a deep sleep and thrown into a pure light.

I came here four years ago. I had not planned to stay, but I couldn't   8
make myself leave. John, the sheepman, put me to work immediately. It was spring, and shearing time. For fourteen days of fourteen hours

each, we moved thousands of sheep through sorting corrals to be sheared, branded, and deloused. I suspect that my original motive for coming here was to "lose myself" in new and unpopulated territory. Instead of producing the numbness I thought I wanted, life on the sheep ranch woke me up. The vitality of the people I was working with flushed out what had become a hallucinatory rawness inside me. I threw away my clothes and bought new ones; I cut my hair. The arid country was a clean slate. Its absolute indifference steadied me.

Sagebrush covers 58,000 squares miles of Wyoming. The biggest 9 city has a population of fifty thousand, and there are only five settlements that could be called cities in the whole state. The rest are towns, scattered across the expanse with as much as sixty miles between them, their populations two thousand, fifty, or ten. They are fugitive-looking, perched on a barren, windblown bench, or tagged onto a river or a railroad, or laid out straight in a farming valley with implement stores and a block-long Mormon church. In the eastern part of the state, which slides down into the Great Plains, the new mining settlements are boomtowns, trailer cities, metal knots on flat land.

Despite the desolate look, there's a coziness to living in this state. 10 There are so few people (only 470,000) that ranchers who buy and sell cattle know one another statewide; the kids who choose to go to college usually go to the state's one university in Laramie; hired hands work their way around Wyoming in a lifetime of hirings and firings. And despite the physical separation, people stay in touch, often driving two or three hours to another ranch for dinner.

Seventy-five years ago, when travel was by buckboard or horse- 11 back, cowboys who were temporarily out of work rode the grub line— drifting from ranch to ranch, mending fences or milking cows, and receiving in exchange a bed and meals. Gossip and messages traveled this slow circuit with them, creating an intimacy between ranchers who were three and four weeks' ride apart. One old-time couple I know, whose turn-of-the-century homestead was used by an outlaw gang as a relay station for stolen horses, recall that if you were traveling, desperado or not, any lighted ranch house was a welcome sign. Even now, for someone who lives in a remote spot, arriving at a ranch or coming to town for supplies is cause for celebration. To emerge from isolation can be disorienting. Everything looks bright, new, vivid. After I had been herding sheep for only three days, the sound of the camp tender's pickup flustered me. Longing for human company, I felt a foolish grin take over my face; yet I had to resist an urgent temptation to run and hide.

Things happen suddenly in Wyoming, the change of seasons and 12 weather; for people, the violent swings in and out of isolation. But good-naturedness is concomitant with severity. Friendliness is a tradition. Strangers passing on the road wave hello. A common sight is two pickups stopped side by side far out on a range, on a dirt track winding through the sage. The drivers will share a cigarette, uncap their thermos bottles, and pass a battered cup, steaming with coffee, between windows. These meetings summon up the details of several generations, because, in Wyoming, private histories are largely public knowledge.

Because ranch work is physical and, these days, economic strain, 13 being "at home on the range" is a matter of vigor, self-reliance, and common sense. A person's life is not a series of dramatic events for which he or she is applauded or exiled but a slow accumulation of days, seasons, years, fleshed out by the generational weight of one's family and anchored by a land-bound sense of place.

In most parts of Wyoming, the human population is visibly out- 14 numbered by the animal. Not far from my town of fifty, I rode into a narrow valley and startled a herd of two hundred elk. Eagles look like small people as they eat car-killed deer by the road. Antelope, moving in small, graceful bands, travel at sixty miles an hour, their mouths open as if drinking in the space.

The solitude in which westerners live makes them quiet. They tele- 15 graph thoughts and feelings by the way they tilt their heads and listen; pulling their Stetsons into a steep dive over their eyes, or pigeon-toeing one boot over the other, they lean against a fence with a fat wedge of Copenhagen beneath their lower lips and take in the whole scene. These detached looks of quiet amusement are sometimes cynical, but they can also come from a dry-eyed humility as lucid as the air is clear.

Conversation goes on in what sounds like a private code; a few 16 phrases imply a complex of meanings. Asking directions, you get a curious list of details. While trailing sheep I was told to "ride up to that kinda upturned rock, follow the pink wash, turn left at the dump, and then you'll see the water hole." One friend told his wife on roundup to "turn at the salt lick and the dead cow," which turned out to be a scattering of bones and no salt lick at all.

Sentence structure is shortened to the skin and bones of a thought. 17 Descriptive words are dropped, even verbs; a cowboy looking over a corral full of horses will say to a wrangler, "Which one needs rode?" People hold back their thoughts in what seems to be a dumbfounded silence, then erupt with an excoriating perceptive remark. Language, so compressed, becomes metaphorical. A rancher ended a relationship with one remark: "You're a bad check," meaning bouncing in and out was intolerable, and even coming back would be no good.

What's behind this laconic style is shyness. There is no vocabulary 18 for the subject of feelings. It's not a hangdog shyness, or anything coy—always there's a robust spirit in evidence behind the restraint, as if the earth-dredging wind that pulls across Wyoming had carried its people's voices away but everything else in them had shouldered confidently into the breeze.

I've spent hours riding to sheep camp at dawn in a pickup when   19
nothing was said; eaten meals in the cookhouse when the only words
spoken were a mumbled "Thank you, ma'am" at the end of dinner.
The silence is profound. Instead of talking, we seem to share one eye.
Keenly observed, the world is transformed. The landscape is engorged
with detail, every movement on it chillingly sharp. The air between
people is charged. Days unfold, bathed in their own music. Nights become hallucinatory; dreams, prescient. . . .

At night, by moonlight, the land is whittled to slivers—a ridge, a   20
river, a strip of grassland stretching to the mountains, then the huge
sky. One morning a full moon was setting in the west just as the sun
was rising. I felt precariously balanced between the two as I loped
across a meadow. For a moment, I could believe that the stars, which
were still visible, work like cooper's band, holding together everything
above Wyoming.

Space has a spiritual equivalent and can heal what is divided and   21
burdensome in us. My grandchildren will probably use space shuttles
for a honeymoon trip or to recover from heart attacks, but closer to
home we might also learn how to carry space inside ourselves in the
effortless way we carry our skins. Space represents sanity, not a life
purified, dull, or "spaced out" but one that might accommodate intel-
ligently any idea or situation.

From the clayey soil of northern Wyoming is mined bentonite,   22
which is used as a filler in candy, gum, and lipstick. We Americans are
great on fillers, as if what we have, what we are, is not enough.
We have a cultural tendency toward denial, but, being affluent, we
strangle ourselves with what we can buy. We have only to look at the
houses we build to see how we build *against* space, the way we drink
against pain and loneliness. We fill up space as if it were a pie shell,
with things whose opacity further obstructs our ability to see what is
already there.

QUESTIONS FOR DISCUSSIONS

1 What impression of Wyoming does the first section of this essay
   give you?
2 Why did Ehrlich come to Wyoming? How has Wyoming changed
   her?
3 How do people in Wyoming take account of their lives? How
   do they feel about one another, about their communities, and
   about isolation? What is the dark side to the grandeur of their
   spaces?
4 How does the way that people use language in Wyoming reflect
   the sense of place there?

5   What is the relationship between open space and values in Wyo-
    ming? How was Wyoming changed by the pioneers and business-
    men? How does Ehrlich explain the American tendency to miss
    the power of space? Explain why you agree or disagree with her.

IDEAS FOR WRITING

1   Write an essay that defines a landscape's character, as Ehrlich
    does here.

2   In a reflective essay, explore Ehrlich's belief that "space has a spir-
    itual equivalent and can heal what is divided and burdensome
    in us."

The Stone Horse

BARRY LOPEZ

*Barry Lopez (b. 1945) was born in New York and spent his youth
in New York and southern California. He received his B.A. and M.A.T.
degrees from Notre Dame University and did his graduate work at
the University of Oregon. Lopez has lived in rural Oregon since 1970.
Like Henry David Thoreau, John Muir, and Gary Snyder (whose essay
"The Etiquette of Freedom" is included in the last section of this
book), he believes in the spiritual power of wild animals and sees
nature as a larger community embracing the human community.
Lopez, a contributing editor to* Harper's *and* North American Review,
*has received many awards for his writing, including the National
Book Award and the John Burroughs Medal. Some of his most widely
read works are* Winter Count *(1981),* Arctic Dreams *(1986),* Crossing
Open Ground *(1988), and* Crow and Weasel *(1990). In the following
selection, he shows how art, history, and spirit intermingle in the
desert of the Southwest.*

The deserts of southern California, the high, relatively cooler and   1
wetter Mojave and the hotter, drier Sonoran to the south of it, carry
the signatures of many cultures. Prehistoric rock drawings in the
Mojave's Coso Range, probably the greatest concentration of petro-
glyphs in North America, are at least three thousand years old. Big
game hunting cultures that flourished six or seven thousand years before that are known from broken spear tips, choppers, and burins left
scattered along the shores of great Pleistocene lakes, long since evaporated. Weapons and tools discovered at China Lake may be thirty
thousand years old; and worked stone from a quarry in the Calico
Mountains is, some argue, evidence that human beings were here
more than two hundred thousand years ago.

Because of the long-term stability of such arid environments, much   2
of this prehistoric stone evidence still lies exposed on the ground,
accessible to anyone who passes by—the studious, the acquisitive, the
indifferent, the merely curious. Archaeologists do not agree on the
sequence of cultural history beyond about twelve thousand years ago,
but it is clear that these broken bits of chalcedony, chert, and obsidian,
like the animal drawings and geometric designs etched on walls of
basalt throughout the desert, anchor the earliest threads of human
history, the first record of human endeavor here.

Western man did not enter the California desert until the end of the   3
eighteenth century, 250 years after Coronado brought his soldiers into
the Zuni pueblos in a bewildered search for the cities of Cibola. The
earliest appraisals of the land were cursory, hurried. People traveled
through it, en route to Santa Fe or the California coastal settlements.

Only miners tarried. In 1823 what had been Spain's became Mexico's
and in 1848 what had been Mexico's became America's; but the bare,
jagged mountains and dry lake beds, the vast and uniform plains of
creosote bush and yucca plants, remained as obscure as the northern
Sudan until the end of the nineteenth century.

Before 1940 the tangible evidence of twentieth-century man's pas-   4
sage here consisted of very little—the hard tracery of travel corridors;
the widely scattered, relatively insignificant evidence of mining operations; and the fair expanse of irrigated fields at the desert's periphery.
In the space of a hundred years or so the wagon roads were paved,
railroads were laid down, and canals and high-tension lines were built
to bring water and electricity across the desert to Los Angeles from the
Colorado River. The dark mouths of gold, talc, and tin mines yawned
from the bony flanks of desert ranges. Dust-encrusted chemical plants
stood at work on the lonely edges of dry lake beds. And crops of grapes,
lettuce, dates, alfalfa, and cotton covered the Coachella and Imperial
valleys, north and south of the Salton Sea, and the Palo Verde Valley
along the Colorado.

These developments proceeded with little or no awareness of   5
earlier human occupations by cultures that preceded those of the historic Indians—the Mohave, the Chemehuevi, the Quechan. (Extensive
irrigation began to actually change the climate of the Sonoran Desert,
and human settlements, the railroads, and farming introduced many
new, successful plants and animals into the region.)

During World War II, the American military moved into the desert in   6
great force, to train troops and to test equipment. They found the clear
weather conducive to year-round flying, the dry air, and isolation very
attractive. After the war, a complex of training grounds, storage facili-
ties, and gunnery and test ranges was permanently settled on more
than three million acres of military reservations. Few perceived the
extent or significance of the destruction of aboriginal sites that took
place during tank maneuvers and bombing runs or in the laying out of
highways, railroads, mining districts, and irrigated fields. The few who
intuited that something like an American Dordogne Valley lay exposed
here were (only) amateur archaeologists; even they reasoned that the
desert was too vast for any of this to matter.

After World War II, people began moving out of the crowded Los   7
Angeles basin into homes in Lucerne, Apple, and Antelope valleys in
the western Mojave. They emigrated as well to a stretch of resort land
at the foot of the San Jacinto Mountains that included Palm Springs,
and farther out to old railroad and military towns like Twentynine
Palms and Barstow. People also began exploring the desert, at first in
military-surplus jeeps and then with a variety of all-terrain and off-
road vehicles that became available in the 1960s. By the mid-1970s,
the number of people using such vehicles for desert recreation had
increased exponentially. Most came and went in innocent curiosity;

the few who didn't wreaked a havoc all out of proportion to their numbers. The disturbance of previously isolated archaeological sites increased by an order of magnitude. Many sites were vandalized before archaeologists, themselves late to the desert, had any firm grasp of the bounds of human history in the desert. It was as though in the same moment an Aztec library had been discovered intact various lacunae had begun to appear.

The vandalism was of three sorts: the general disturbance usually   8
caused by souvenir hunters and by the curious and the oblivious; the wholesale stripping of a place by professional thieves for black-market sale and trade; and outright destruction, in which vehicles were actually used to tarn and trench an area. By 1980, the Bureau of Land Management [BLM] estimated that probably thirty-five percent of the archaeological sites in the desert had been vandalized. The destruction at some places by rifles and shotguns, or by power winches mounted on vehicles, was, if one cared for history, demoralizing to behold.

In spite of public education, land closures, and stricter law en-   9
forcement in recent years, the BLM estimates that, annually, about one percent of the archaeological record in the desert continues to be destroyed or stolen.

II

A BLM archaeologist told me, with understandable reluctance,   10
where to find the intaglio. I spread my Automobile Club of Southern California map of Imperial County out on his desk, and he traced the route with a pink felt-tip pen. The line crossed Interstate 8 and then turned west along the Mexican border.

"You can't drive any farther than about here," he said, marking a   11
small *x*. "There's boulders in the wash. You walk up past them."

On a separate piece of paper he drew a route in a smaller scale that   12
would take me up the arroyo to a certain point where I was to cross back east, to another arroyo. At its head, on higher ground just to the north, I would find the horse.

"It's tough to spot unless you know it's there. Once you pick it up . . ."   13
He shook his head slowly, in a gesture of wonder at its existence.

I waited until I held his eye. I assured him I would not tell anyone   14
else how to get there. He looked at me with stoical despair, like a man who had been robbed twice, whose belief in human beings was offered without conviction.

I did not go until the following day because I wanted to see it at   15
dawn. I ate breakfast at 4 A.M. in El Centro and then drove south. The route was easy to follow, though the last section of road proved difficult, broken and drifted over with sand in some spots. I came to the barricade of boulders and parked. It was light enough by then to find

my way over the ground with little trouble. The contours of the land-scape were stark, without any masking vegetation. I worried only about rattlesnakes.

I traversed the stone plain as directed, but, in spite of the frankness   16
of the land, I came on the horse unawares. In the first moment of recognition I was without feeling. I recalled later being startled, and that I held my breath. It was laid out on the ground with its head to the east, three times life size. As I took in its outline I felt a growing con-centration of all my senses, as though my attentiveness to the pale rose color of the morning sky and other peripheral images had now ceased to be important. I was aware that I was straining for sound in the windless air and I felt the uneven pressure of the earth hard against my feet. The horse, outlined in a standing profile on the dark ground, was as vivid before me as a bed of tulips.

I've come upon animals suddenly before, and felt a similar tension,   17
a precipitate heightening of the senses. And I have felt the inexplic-able but sharply boosted intensity of a wild moment in the bush, where it is not until some minutes later that you discover the source of electricity—the warm remains of a grizzly bear kill, or the still moist tracks of a wolverine.

But this was slightly different. I felt I had stepped into an unoccu-   18
pied corridor. I had no familiar sense of history, the temporal struc-ture in which to think. This horse was made by Quechan people three hundred years ago. I felt instead a headlong rush of images: people hunting wild horses with spears on the Pleistocene veld of southern California; Cortés riding across the causeway into Montezuma's Tenochtitlán; a short-legged Comanche, astride his horse like some sort of ferret, slashing through cavalry lines of young men who rode like farmers. A hoof exploding past my face one morning in a corral in Wyoming. These images had the weight and silence of stone.

When I released my breath, the images softened. My initial feeling,   19
of facing a wild animal in a remote region, was replaced with a calm sense of antiquity. It was then that I became conscious, like an ordi-nary tourist, of what was before me, and thought: This horse was probably laid out by Quechan people. But when, I wondered? The first horses they saw, I knew, might have been those that came north from Mexico in 1692 with Father Eusebio Kino. But Cocopa people, I recalled, also came this far north on occasion, to fight with the neigh-bors, the Quechan. And *they* could have seen horses with Melchior Díaz, at the mouth of the Colorado River in the fall of 1540. So, it could be four hundred years old. (No one in fact knows.)

I still had not moved. I took my eyes off the horse for a moment to   20
look south over the desert plain into Mexico, to look east past its head at the brightening sunrise, to situate myself. Then, finally, I brought my trailing foot slowly forward and stood erect. Sunlight was running like a thin sheet of water over the stony ground and it threw the horse

into relief. It looked as though no hand had ever disturbed the stones that gave it its form.

The horse had been brought to life on ground called desert pave-   21 ment, a tight, flat matrix of small cobbles blasted smooth by sand-laden winds. The uniform, monochromatic blackness of the stones, a patina of iron and magnesium oxides called desert varnish, is caused by long-term exposure to the sun. To make this type of low-relief ground glyph, or intaglio, the artist either selectively turns individual stones over to their lighter side or removes areas of stone to expose the lighter soil underneath, creating a negative image. This horse, about eighteen feet from brow to rump and eight feet from withers to hoof, had been made in the latter way, and its outline was bermed at certain points with low ridges of stone a few inches high to enhance its three-dimensional qualities. (The left side of the horse was in full profile; each leg was extended at 90 degrees to the body and fully visible, as though seen in three-quarter profile.)

I was not eager to move. The moment I did I would be back in the   22 flow of time, the horse no longer quivering in the same way before me. I did not want to feel again the sequence of quotidian events—to be drawn off into deliberation and analysis. A human being, a four-footed animal, the open land. That was all that was present—and a "thoughtless" understanding of the very old desires beating on this particular animal: to hunt it, to render it, to fathom it, to subjugate it, to honor it, to take it as a companion.

What finally made me move was the light. The sun now filled the   23 shallow basin of the horse's body. The weighted line of the stone berm created the illusion of a mane and the distinctive roundness of an equine belly. The change in definition impelled me. I moved to the left, circling past its rump, to see how the light might flesh the horse out from various points of view. I circled it completely before squatting on my haunches. Ten or fifteen minutes later I chose another view. The third time I moved, to a point near the rear hooves, I spotted a stone tool at my feet. I stared at it a long while, more in awe than disbelief, before reaching out to pick it up. I turned it over in my left palm and took it between my fingers to feel its cutting edge. It is always difficult, especially with something so portable, to rechannel the desire to steal.

I spent several hours with the horse. As I changed positions and as   24 the angle of the light continued to change I noticed a number of things. The angle at which the pastern carried the hoof away from the ankle was perfect. Also, stones had been placed within the image to suggest, at precisely the right spot, the left shoulder above the foreleg. The line that joined thigh and hock was similarly accurate. The muzzle alone seemed distorted—but perhaps these stones had been moved by a later hand. It was an admirably accurate representation, but not what a breeder would call perfect conformation. There was the

suggestion of a bowed neck and an undershot jaw, and the tail, as full
as a winter coyote's, did not appear to be precisely to scale.

The more I thought about it, the more I felt I was looking at an in-   25
dividual horse, a unique combination of genetic and specific detail. It
was easy to imagine one of Kino's horses as a model, or a horse that
ran off from one of Coronado's columns. What kind of horses would
these have been, I wondered? In the sixteenth century the most sought-
after horses in Europe were Spanish, the offspring of Arabian stock
and Barbary horses that the Moors brought to Iberia and bred to the
older, eastern European strains brought in by the Romans. The model
for this horse, I speculated, could easily have been a palomino, or a
descendant of horses trained for lion-hunting in North Africa.

A few generations ago, cowboys, cavalry quartermasters, and dray-   26
men would have taken this horse before me under consideration and
not let up their scrutiny until they had its heritage fixed to their satis-
faction. Today, the distinction between draft and harness horses is ar-
cane knowledge, and no image may come to mind for a blue roan or a
claybank horse. The loss of such refinement in everyday conversation
leaves me unsettled. People praise the Eskimo's ability to distinguish
among forty types of snow but forget the skill of others who routinely
differentiate between overo and tobiano pintos. Such distinctions are
made for the same reason. You have to do it to be able to talk clearly
about the world.

For parts of two years I worked as a horse wrangler and packer in   27
Wyoming. It is dim knowledge now; I would have to think to remember
if a buckskin was a kind of dun horse. And I couldn't throw a double-
diamond hitch over a set of panniers—the packer's basic tie-down—
without guidance. As I squatted there in the desert, however, these
more personal memories seemed tenuous in comparison with the
sweep of this animal in human time. My memories had no depth. I
thought of the Hittite cavalry riding against the Syrians 3500 years
ago. And the first of the Chinese emperors, Ch'in Shih Huang, buried
in Shensi Province in 210 B.C. with thousands of life-size horses and
soldiers, a terra-cotta guardian army. What could I know of what was
in the mind of whoever made this horse? Was there some racial memory of it as an animal that had once fed the artist's ancestors and then
disappeared from North America? And then returned in this strange
alliance with another race of men?

Certainly, whoever it was, the artist had observed the animal very   28
closely. Certainly the animal's speed had impressed him. Among the
first things the Quechan would have learned from an encounter with
Kino's horses was that their own long-distance runners—men who
could run down mule deer—were no match for this animal.

From where I squatted I could look far out over the Mexican plain.   29
Juan Bautista de Anza passed this way in 1774, extending El Camino
Real into Alta California from Sinaloa. He was followed by others, all

of them astride the magical horse; *gente de razón,* the people of reason, coming into the country of *los primitivos.* The horse, like the stone animals of Egypt, urged these memories upon me. And as I drew them up from some forgotten corner of my mind—huge horses carved in the white chalk downs of southern England by an Iron Age people; Spanish horses rearing and wheeling in fear before alligators in Florida—the images seemed tethered before me. With this sense of proportion, a memory of my own—the morning I almost lost my face to a horse's hoof—now had somewhere to fit.

I rose up and began to walk slowly around the horse again. I had   30
taken the first long measure of it and was looking now for a way to de-part, a new angle of light, a fading of the image itself before the rising sun, that would break its hold on me. As I circled, feeling both heady and serene at the encounter, I realized again how strangely vivid it was. It had been created on a barren bajada between two arroyos, as nondescript a place as one could imagine. The only plant life here was a few wands of ocotillo cactus. The ground beneath my shoes was so hard it wouldn't take the print of a heavy animal even after a rain. The only sounds I had heard here were the voices of quail.

The archaeologist had been correct. For all its forcefulness, the   31
horse is inconspicuous. If you don't care to see it you can walk right past it. That pleases him, I think. Unmarked on this bleak shoulder of the plain, the site signals to no one; so he wants no protective fences here, no informative plaque, to act as beacons. He would rather take a chance that no motorcyclist, no aimless wanderer with a flair for violence and a depth of ignorance, will ever find his way here.

The archaeologist had given me something before I left his office   32
that now seemed peculiar—an aerial photograph of the horse. It is widely believed that an aerial view of an intaglio provides a fair and accurate description. It does not. In the photograph the horse looks somewhat crudely constructed; from the ground it appears far more deftly rendered. The photograph is of a single moment, and in that split second the horse seems vaguely impotent. I watched light pool in the intaglio at dawn; I imagine you could watch it withdraw at dusk and sense the same animation I did. In those prolonged moments its shape and so, too, its general character changed—noticeably. The living quality of the image, its immediacy to the eye, was brought out by the light-in-time, not, at least here, in the camera's frozen instant.

Intaglios, I thought, were never meant to be seen by gods in the sky   33
above. They were meant to be seen by people on the ground, over a long period of shifting light. This could even be true of the huge figures on the Plain of Nazca in Peru, where people could walk for the length of a day beside them. It is our own impatience that leads us to think otherwise.

This process of abstraction, almost unintentional, drew me gradu-   34
ally away from the horse. I came to a position of attention at the edge

of the sphere of its influence. With a slight bow I paid my respects to the horse, its maker, and the history of us all, and departed.

III

A short distance away I stopped the car in the middle of the road to make a few notes. I had not been able to write down what I was thinking when I was with the horse. It would have seemed disrespectful, and it would have required another kind of attention. So now I patiently drained my memory of the details it had fastened itself upon. The road I'd stopped on was adjacent to the All American Canal, the major source of water for the Imperial and Coachella valleys. The water flowed west placidly. A disjointed flock of coots, small, dark birds with white bills, was paddling against the current, foraging in the rushes.   35

I was peripherally aware of the birds as I wrote, the only movement in the desert; and of a series of sounds from a village a half-mile away. The first sounds from this collection of ramshackle houses in a grove of cottonwoods were the distracted dawn voices of dogs. I heard them intermingled with the cries of a rooster. Later, the high-pitched voices of children calling out to each other came disembodied through the dry desert air. Now, a little after seven, I could hear someone practicing on the trumpet, the same rough phrases played over and over. I suddenly remembered how as children we had tried to get the rhythm of a galloping horse with hands against our thighs, or by fluttering our tongues against the roofs of our mouths.   36

After the trumpet, the impatient calls of adults, summoning children. Sunday morning. Wood smoke hung like a lens in the trees. The first car starts—a cold, eight-cylinder engine, of Chrysler extraction perhaps, goosed to life, then throttled back to murmur through dual mufflers, the obbligato music of a shade-tree mechanic. The rote bark of mongrel dogs at dawn, then jagged outcries of men and women, an engine coming to life. Like a thousand villages from West Virginia to Guadalajara.   37

I finished my notes—where was I going to find a description of the horses that came north with the conquistadors? Did their manes come forward prominently over the brow, like this one's, like the forelocks of Blackfeet and Assiniboine men in nineteenth-century paintings? I set the notes on the seat beside me.   38

The road followed the canal for a while and then arced north, toward Interstate 8. It was slow driving and I fell to thinking how the desert had changed since Anza had come through. New plants and animals—the MacDougall cottonwood, the English house sparrow, the chukar from India—have about them now the air of the native-born. Of the native species, some—no one knows how many—are extinct. The populations of many others, especially the animals, have been sharply reduced. The   39

idea of a desert impoverished by agricultural poisons and varmint
hunters, by off-road vehicles and military operations, did not seem as
disturbing to me, however, as this other horror, now that I had been
those hours with the horse. The vandals, the few who crowbar rock art
off the desert's walls, who dig up graves, who punish the ground that
holds intaglios, are people who devour history. Their self-centered
scorn, their disrespect for ideas and images beyond their ken, create
the awful atmosphere of loose ends in which totalitarianism thrives, in
which the past is merely curious or wrong.

   I thought about the horse sitting out there on the unprotected plain.   40
I enumerated its qualities in my mind until a sense of its vulnerability
receded and it became an anchor for something else. I remembered
that history, a history like this one, which ran deeper than Mexico,
deeper than the Spanish, was a kind of medicine. It permitted the great
breadth of human expression to reverberate, and it did not urge you to
locate its apotheosis in the present.

   Each of us, individuals and civilizations, has been held upside   41
down like Achilles in the River Styx. The artist mixing his colors in the
dim light of Altamira; an Egyptian ruler lying still now, wrapped in his
byssus, stored against time in a pyramid; the faded Dorset culture of
the Arctic; the Hmong and Samburu and Walbiri of historic time; the
modern nations. This great, imperfect stretch of human expression is
the clarification and encouragement, the urging and the reminder, we
call history. And it is inscribed everywhere in the face of the land, from
the mountain passes of the Himalayas to a nameless bajada in the
California desert.

   Small birds rose up in the road ahead, startled, and flew off. I prayed   42
no infidel would ever find that horse.

| QUESTIONS FOR DISCUSSION |

 1 Lopez refers to the desert area outside of the Los Angeles basin and
    extending towards Colorado as the American Dordogne Valley. In
    what ways is this area similar to the Dordogne Valley in the south
    of France? When and why did the Bureau of Land Management
    become protective of this area?

 2 Why is the Stone Horse an "intaglio"? Explain Lopez's first re-
    sponses to the Stone Horse. Did his description evoke memories
    of experiences you have had in natural or archaeological sites?
    Discuss your answer.

 3 Why is the aerial view of the Stone Horse inadequate and
    misrepresentative?

 4 Lopez is unable to write about the Stone Horse in its presence.
    Why?

5   In what ways has Lopez's journey been healing? Why does he
    pray that "no infidel would ever find that horse"? What do you
    think Lopez means when he concludes, "Each of us, individuals
    and civilizations, has been held upside down like Achilles in the
    River Styx"?

IDEAS FOR WRITING

1   Spend several hours at an archaeological site, and then write
    an essay that captures the ideas and feelings you had while you
    were there.

2   Write an essay in which you explain both what you think the Stone
    Horse represents to Lopez and what meaning it has for you.

Total Eclipse

ANNIE DILLARD

Poet, essayist, novelist, and naturalist, Annie Dillard (b. 1945) was raised in Pittsburgh, Pennsylvania. She received a B.A. in 1968 from Hollins College in Virginia. Dillard has worked as an editor and has been the writer in residence at Wesleyan College in Connecticut for a number of years. She is best known for her essays and books about writing and nature. In 1974 Dillard was awarded the Pulitzer Prize for her first book, Pilgrim at Tinker Creek. *The autobiography of her early years is entitled* An American Childhood *(1987). Her other books include* Holy the Firm *(1978),* Living by Fiction *(1982), and* Mornings Like This: Found Poems *(1995). "Total Eclipse," which is included in* Teaching a Stone to Talk *(1982), captures the mysterious, intense, and enduring power of the sun.*

I

It had been like dying, that sliding down the mountain pass. It had   1
been like the death of someone, irrational, that sliding down the mountain pass and into the region of dread. It was like slipping into fever, or falling down that hole in sleep from which you wake yourself whimpering. We had crossed the mountains that day, and now we were in a strange place—a hotel in central Washington, in a town near Yakima. The eclipse we had traveled here to see would occur early the next morning.

I lay in bed. My husband, Gary, was reading beside me. I lay in bed   2
and looked at the painting on the hotel room wall. It was a print of a detailed and lifelike painting of a smiling clown's head, made out of vegetables. It was a painting of the sort which you do not intend to look at, and which, alas, you never forget. Some tasteless fate presses it upon you; it becomes part of the complex interior junk you carry with you wherever you go. Two years have passed since the total eclipse of which I write. During those years I have forgotten, I assume, a great many things I wanted to remember—but I have not forgotten that clown painting or its lunatic setting in the old hotel.

The clown was bald. Actually, he wore a clown's tight rubber wig,   3
painted white; this stretched over the top of his skull, which was a cabbage. His hair was bunches of baby carrots. Inset in his white clown makeup, and in his cabbage skull, were his small and laughing human eyes. The clown's glance was like the glance of Rembrandt in some of the self-portraits: lively, knowing, deep, and loving. The crinkled shadows around his eyes were string beans. His eyebrows

were parsley. Each of his ears was a broad bean. His thin, joyful lips were red chili peppers; between his lips were wet rows of human teeth and a suggestion of a real tongue. The clown print was framed in gilt and glassed.

To put ourselves in the path of the total eclipse, that day we had   4
driven five hours inland from the Washington coast, where we lived. When we tried to cross the Cascades range, an avalanche had blocked the pass.

A slope's worth of snow blocked the road; traffic backed up. Had the   5
avalanche buried any cars that morning? We could not learn. This highway was the only winter road over the mountains. We waited as highway crews bulldozed a passage through the avalanche. With two-by-fours and walls of plyboard, they erected a one-way, roofed tunnel through the avalanche. We drove through the avalanche tunnel, crossed the pass, and descended several thousand feet into central Washington and the broad Yakima valley, about which we knew only that it was orchard country. As we lost altitude, the snows disappeared; our ears popped; the trees changed, and in the trees were strange birds. I watched the landscape innocently, like a fool, like a diver in the rapture of the deep who plays on the bottom while his air runs out.

The hotel lobby was a dark, derelict room, narrow as a corridor, and   6
seemingly without air. We waited on a couch while the manager vanished upstairs to do something unknown to our room. Beside us on an overstuffed chair, absolutely motionless, was a platinum-blond woman in her forties wearing a black silk dress and a strand of pearls. Her long legs were crossed; she supported her head on her fist. At the dim far end of the room, their backs toward us, sat six bald old men in their shirtsleeves, around a loud television. Two of them seemed asleep. They were drunks. "Number six!" cried the man on television, "Number six!"

On the broad lobby desk, lighted and bubbling, was a ten-gallon   7
aquarium containing one large fish; the fish tilted up and down in its water. Against the long opposite wall sang a live canary in its cage. Beneath the cage, among spilled millet seeds on the carpet, were a decorated child's sand bucket and matching sand shovel.

Now the alarm was set for six. I lay awake remembering an article   8
I had read downstairs in the lobby, in an engineering magazine. The article was about gold mining.

In South Africa, in India, and in South Dakota, the gold mines ex-   9
tend so deeply into the earth's crust that they are hot. The rock walls burn the miners' hands. The companies have to air-condition the mines; if the air conditioners break, the miners die. The elevators in the mine shafts run very slowly, down, and up, so the miners' ears will

not pop in their skulls. When the miners return to the surface, their faces are deathly pale.

Early the next morning we checked out. It was February 26, 1979, a Monday morning. We would drive out of town, find a hilltop, watch the eclipse, and then drive back over the mountains and home to the coast. How familiar things are here; how adept we are; how smoothly and professionally we check out! I had forgotten the clown's smiling head and the hotel lobby as if they had never existed. Gary put the car in gear and off we went, as off we have gone to a hundred other adventures.   10

It was before dawn when we found a highway out of town and drove into the unfamiliar countryside. By the growing light we could see a band of cirrostratus clouds in the sky. Later the rising sun would clear these clouds before the eclipse began. We drove at random until we came to a range of unfenced hills. We pulled off the highway, bundled up, and climbed one of these hills.   11

II

The hill was five hundred feet high. Long winter-killed grass covered it, as high as our knees. We climbed and rested, sweating in the cold; we passed clumps of bundled people on the hillside who were setting up telescopes and fiddling with cameras. The top of the hill stuck up in the middle of the sky. We tightened our scarves and looked around.   12

East of us rose another hill like ours. Between the hills, far below, was the highway which threaded south into the valley. This was the Yakima valley; I had never seen it before. It is justly famous for its beauty, like every planted valley. It extended south into the horizon, a distant dream of a valley, a Shangri-la. All its hundreds of low, golden slopes bore orchards. Among the orchards were towns, and roads, and plowed and fallow fields. Through the valley wandered a thin, shining river; from the river extended fine, frozen irrigation ditches. Distance blurred and blued the sight, so that the whole valley looked like a thickness or sediment at the bottom of the sky. Directly behind us was more sky, and empty lowlands blued by distance, and Mount Adams. Mount Adams was an enormous, snow-covered volcanic cone rising flat, like so much scenery.   13

Now the sun was up. We could not see it; but the sky behind the band of clouds was yellow, and, far down the valley, some hillside orchards had lighted up. More people were parking near the highway and climbing the hills. It was the West. All of us rugged individualists were wearing knit caps and blue nylon parkas. People were climbing   14 the nearby hills and setting up shop in clumps among the dead grasses. It looked as though we had all gathered on hilltops to pray for the world on its last day. It looked as though we had all crawled out of spaceships and were preparing to assault the valley below. It looked as though we were scattered on hilltops at dawn to sacrifice virgins, make rain, set stone stelae in a ring. There was no place out of the wind. The straw grasses banged our legs.

Up in the sky where we stood this air was lusterless yellow. To the   15
west the sky was blue. Now the sun cleared the clouds. We cast rough shadows on the blowing grass; freezing, we waved our arms. Near the sun, the sky was bright and colorless. There was nothing to see.

It began with no ado. It was odd that such a well-advertised public   16
event should have no starting gun, no overture, no introductory speaker. I should have known right then that I was out of my depth. Without pause or preamble, silent as orbits, a piece of the sun went away. We looked at it through welders' goggles. A piece of the sun was missing; in its place we saw empty sky.

I had seen a partial eclipse in 1970. A partial eclipse is very inter-   17
esting. It bears almost no relation to a total eclipse. Seeing a partial eclipse bears the same relation to seeing a total eclipse as kissing a man does to marrying him, or as flying in an airplane does to falling out of an airplane. Although the one experience precedes the other, it in no way prepares you for it. During a partial eclipse the sky does not darken—not even when 94 percent of the sun is hidden. Nor does the sun, seen colorless through protective devices, seem terribly strange. We have all seen a sliver of light in the sky; we have all seen the crescent moon by day. However, during a partial eclipse the air does indeed get cold, precisely as if someone were standing between you and the fire. And blackbirds do fly back to their roosts. I had seen a partial eclipse before, and here was another.

What you see in an eclipse is entirely different from what you   18
know. It is especially different for those of us whose grasp of astron- omy is so frail that, given a flashlight, a grapefruit, two oranges, and fifteen years, we still could not figure out which way to set the clocks for Daylight Saving Time. Usually it is a bit of a trick to keep your knowledge from blinding you. But during an eclipse it is easy. What you see is much more convincing than any wild-eyed theory you may know.

You may read that the moon has something to do with eclipses.   19
I have never seen the moon yet. You do not see the moon. So near the sun, it is as completely invisible as the stars are by day. What you see before your eyes is the sun going through phases. It gets narrower and narrower, as the waning moon does, and, like the ordinary moon, it travels alone in the simple sky. The sky is of course background.

It does not appear to eat the sun; it is far behind the sun. The sun simply shaves away; gradually, you see less sun and more sky.

The sky's blue was deepening, but there was no darkness. The sun   20
was a wide crescent, like a segment of tangerine. The wind freshened and blew steadily over the hill. The eastern hill across the highway grew dusky and sharp. The towns and orchards in the valley to the south were dissolving into the blue light. Only the thin river held a trickle of sun.

Now the sky to the west deepened to indigo, a color never seen. A   21
dark sky usually loses color. This was a saturated, deep indigo, up in the air. Stuck up into that unwordly sky was the cone of Mount Adams, and the alpenglow was upon it. The alpenglow is that red light of sunset which holds out on snowy mountaintops long after the valleys and tablelands are dimmed. "Look at Mount Adams," I said, and that was the last sane moment I remember.

I turned back to the sun. It was going. The sun was going, and the   22
world was wrong. The grasses were wrong; they were platinum. Their every detail of stem, head, and blade shone lightless and artificially distinct as an art photographer's platinum print. This color has never been seen on earth. The hues were metallic; their finish was matte. The hillside was a nineteenth-century tinted photograph from which the tints had faded. All the people you see in the photograph, distinct and detailed as their faces look, are now dead. The sky was navy blue. My hands were silver. All the distant hills' grasses were finespun metal which the wind laid down. I was watching a faded color print of a movie filmed in the Middle Ages; I was standing in it, by some mistake. I was standing in a movie of hillside grasses filmed in the Middle Ages. I missed my own century, the people I knew, and the real light of day.

I looked at Gary. He was in the film. Everything was lost. He was a   23
platinum print, a dead artist's version of life. I saw on his skull the darkness of night mixed with the colors of day. My mind was going out; my eyes were receding the way galaxies recede to the rim of space. Gary was light-years away, gesturing inside a circle of darkness, down the wrong end of a telescope. He smiled as if he saw me; the stringy crinkles around his eyes moved. The sight of him, familiar and wrong, was something I was remembering from centuries hence, from the other side of death: yes, *that* is the way he used to look, when we were living. When it was our generation's turn to be alive. I could not hear him; the wind was too loud. Behind him the sun was going. We had all started down a chute of time. At first it was pleasant; now there was no stopping it. Gary was chuting away across space, moving and talking and catching my eye, chuting down the long corridor of separation. The skin on his face moved like thin bronze plating that would peel.

The grass at our feet was wild barley. It was the wild einkorn wheat   24
which grew on the hilly flanks of the Zagros Mountains, above the
Euphrates valley, above the valley of the river we called *River.* We har-
vested the grass with stone sickles, I remember. We found the grasses
on the hillsides; we built our shelter beside them and cut them down.
That is how he used to look then, that one, moving and living and
catching my eye, with the sky so dark behind him, and the wind blowing. God save our life.

From all the hills came screams. A piece of sky beside the crescent   25
sun was detaching. It was a loosened circle of evening sky, suddenly
lighted from the back. It was an abrupt black body out of nowhere; it
was a flat disk; it was almost over the sun. That is when there were
screams. At once this disk of sky slid over the sun like a lid. The sky
snapped over the sun like a lens cover. The hatch in the brain
slammed. Abruptly it was dark night, on the land and in the sky. In the
night sky was a tiny ring of light. The hole where the sun belongs is very
small. A thin ring of light marked its place. There was no sound. The
eyes dried, the arteries drained, the lungs hushed. There was no world.
We were the world's dead people rotating and orbiting around and
around, embedded in the planet's crust, while the earth rolled down.
Our minds were light-years distant, forgetful of almost everything.
Only an extraordinary act of will could recall to us our former, living
selves and our contexts in matter and time. We had, it seems, loved the
planet and loved our lives, but could no longer remember the way of
them. We got the light wrong. In the sky was something that should not
be there. In the black sky was a ring of light. It was a thin ring, an old,
thin silver wedding band, an old, worn ring. It was an old wedding
band in the sky, or a morsel of bone. There were stars. It was all over.

III

It is now that the temptation is strongest to leave these regions. We   26
have seen enough; let's go. Why burn our hands any more than we
have to? But two years have passed; the price of gold has risen. I return
to the same buried alluvial beds and pick through the strata again.

I saw, early in the morning, the sun diminish against a backdrop of   27
sky. I saw a circular piece of that sky appear, suddenly detached, blackened, and backlighted; from nowhere it came and overlapped the sun.
It did not look like the moon. It was enormous and black. If I had not
read that it was the moon, I could have seen the sight a hundred times
and never thought of the moon once. (If, however, I had not read that
it was the moon—if, like most of the world's people throughout time,
I had simply glanced up and seen this thing—then I doubtless would
not have speculated much, but would have, like Emperor Louis of

Bavaria in 840, simply died of fright on the spot.) It did not look like a dragon, although it looked more like a dragon than the moon. It looked like a lens cover, or the lid of a pot. It materialized out of thin air—black, and flat, and sliding, outlined in flame.

Seeing this black body was like seeing a mushroom cloud. The heart   28
screeched. The meaning of the sight overwhelmed its fascination. It obliterated meaning itself. If you were to glance out one day and see a row of mushroom clouds rising on the horizon, you would know at once that what you were seeing, remarkable as it was, was intrinsically not worth remarking. No use running to tell anyone. Significant as it was, it did not matter a whit. For what is significance? It is significance for people. No people, no significance. This is all I have to tell you.

In the deeps are the violence and terror of which psychology has   29
warned us. But if you ride these monsters deeper down, if you drop with them farther over the world's rim, you find what our sciences cannot locate or name, the substrate, the ocean or matrix or ether which buoys the rest, which gives goodness its power for good, and evil its power for evil, the unified field: our complex and inexplicable caring for each other, and for our life together here. This is given. It is not learned.

The world which lay under darkness and stillness following the   30
closing of the lid was not the world we know. The event was over. Its devastation lay round about us. The clamoring mind and heart stilled, almost indifferent, certainly disembodied, frail, and exhausted. The hills were hushed, obliterated. Up in the sky, like a crater from some distant cataclysm, was a hollow ring.

You have seen photographs of the sun taken during a total eclipse.   31
The corona fills the print. All of those photographs were taken through telescopes. The lenses of telescopes and cameras can no more cover the breadth and scale of the visual array than language can cover the breadth and simultaneity of internal experience. Lenses enlarge the sight, omit its context, and make of it a pretty and sensible picture, like something on a Christmas card. I assure you, if you send any shepherds a Christmas card on which is printed a three-by-three photograph of the angel of the Lord, the glory of the Lord, and a multitude of the heavenly host, they will not be sore afraid. More fearsome things can come in envelopes. More moving photographs than those of the sun's corona can appear in magazines. But I pray you will never see anything more awful in the sky.

You see the wide world swaddled in darkness; you see a vast   32
breadth of hilly land, and an enormous, distant, blackened valley; you see towns' lights, a river's path, and blurred portions of your hat and scarf; you see your husband's face looking like an early black-and-white film; and you see a sprawl of black sky and blue sky together, with unfamiliar stars in it, some barely visible bands of cloud, and over there, a small white ring. The ring is as small as one goose in a flock of migrating geese—if you happen to notice a flock of migrating

geese. It is one 360th part of the visible sky. The sun we see is less than half the diameter of a dime held at arm's length.

The Crab Nebula, in the constellation Taurus, looks, through 33 binoculars, like a smoke ring. It is a star in the process of exploding. Light from its explosion first reached the earth in 1054; it was a super-nova then, and so bright it shone in the daytime. Now it is not so bright, but it is still exploding. It expands at the rate of seventy million miles a day. It is interesting to look through binoculars at something expanding seventy million miles a day. It does not budge. Its apparent size does not increase. Photographs of the Crab Nebula taken fifteen years ago seem identical to photographs of it taken yesterday. Some lichens are similar. Botanists have measured some ordinary lichens twice, at fifty-year intervals, without detecting any growth at all. And yet their cells divide; they live.

The small ring of light was like these things—like a ridiculous 34 lichen up in the sky, like a perfectly still explosion 4,200 light-years away: it was interesting, and lovely, and in witless motion, and it had nothing to do with anything.

It had nothing to do with anything. The sun was too small, and too 35 cold, and too far away, to keep the world alive. The white ring was not enough. It was feeble and worthless. It was as useless as a memory; it was as off kilter and hollow and wretched as a memory.

When you try your hardest to recall someone's face, or the look of a 36 place, you see in your mind's eye some vague and terrible sight such as this. It is dark; it is insubstantial; it is all wrong.

The white ring and the saturated darkness made the earth and the 37 sky look as they must look in the memories of the careless dead. What I saw, what I seemed to be standing in, was all the wrecked light that the memories of the dead could shed upon the living world. We had all died in our boots on the hilltops of Yakima, and were alone in eternity. Empty space stoppered our eyes and mouths; we cared for nothing. We remembered our living days wrong. With great effort we had remem-bered some sort of circular light in the sky—but only the outline. Oh, and then the orchard trees withered, the ground froze, the glaciers slid down the valleys and overlapped the towns. If there had ever been people on earth, nobody knew it. The dead had forgotten those they had loved. The dead were parted one from the other and could no longer remember the faces and lands they had loved in the light. They seemed to stand on darkened hilltops, looking down.

IV

We teach our children one thing only, as we were taught: to wake 38 up. We teach our children to look alive there, to join by words and ac-tivities the life of human culture on the planet's crust. As adults we are almost all adept at waking up. We have so mastered the transition we have forgotten we ever learned it. Yet it is a transition we make a hundred times a day, as, like so many will-less dolphins, we plunge and surface, lapse and emerge. We live half our waking lives and all of our sleeping lives in some private, useless, and insensible waters we never mention or recall. Useless, I say. Valueless, I might add—until someone hauls their wealth up to the surface and into the wide-awake city, in a form that people can use.

I do not know how we got to the restaurant. Like Roethke, "I take my waking slow." Gradually I seemed more or less alive, and already forgetful. It was not almost nine in the morning. It was the day of a solar eclipse in central Washington, and a fine adventure for everyone. The sky was clear; there was a fresh breeze out of the north. 39

The restaurant was a roadside place with tables and booths. The other eclipse-watchers were there. From our booth we could see their cars' California license plates, their University of Washington parking stickers. Inside the restaurant we were all eating eggs or waffles; people were fairly shouting and exchanging enthusiasms, like fans after a World Series game. Did you see . . . ? Did you see . . . ? Then somebody said something which knocked me for a loop. 40

A college student, a boy in a blue parka who carried a Hasselblad, said to us, "Did you see that little white ring? It looked like a Life Saver. It looked like a Life Saver up in the sky." 41

And so it did. The boy spoke well. He was a walking alarm clock. I myself had at that time no access to such a word. He could write a sentence, and I could not. I grabbed that Life Saver and rode it to the surface. And I had to laugh. I had been dumbstruck on the Euphrates River, I had been dead and gone and grieving, all over the sight of something which, if you could claw your way up to that level, you would grant looked very much like a Life Saver. It was good to be back among people so clever; it was good to have all the world's words at the mind's disposal, so the mind could begin its task. All those things for which we have no words are lost. The mind—the culture—has two little tools, grammar and lexicon: a decorated sand bucket and a matching shovel. With these we bluster about the continents and do all the world's work. With these we try to save our very lives. 42

There are a few more things to tell from this level, the level of the restaurant. One is the old joke about breakfast. "It can never be satisfied, the mind, never." Wallace Stevens wrote that, and in the long run he was right. The mind wants to live forever, or to learn a very good reason why not. The mind wants the world to return its love, or its awareness; the mind wants to know all the world, and all eternity, and God. The mind's sidekick, however, will settle for two eggs over easy. 43

The dear, stupid body is as easily satisfied as a spaniel. And, incredibly, the simple spaniel can lure the brawling mind to its dish. It is 44

everlastingly funny that the proud, metaphysically ambitious, clamoring mind will hush if you give it an egg.

    Further: while the mind reels in deep space, while the mind grieves   45
or fears or exults, the workaday senses, in ignorance or idiocy, like
so many computer terminals printing out market prices while the
world blows up, still transcribe their little data and transmit them to
the warehouse in the skull. Later, under the tranquilizing influence of
fried eggs, the mind can sort through this data. The restaurant was a
halfway house, a decompression chamber. There I remembered a few
things more.

    The deepest, and most terrifying, was this: I have said that I heard   46
screams. (I have since read that screaming, with hysteria, is a common
reaction even to expected total eclipses.) People on all the hillsides, including, I think, myself, screamed when the black body of the moon
detached from the sky and rolled over the sun. But something else was
happening at the same instant, and it was this, I believe, which made
us scream.

    The second before the sun went out we saw a wall of dark shadow   47
come speeding at us. We no sooner saw it than it was upon us, like
thunder. It roared up the valley. It slammed our hill and knocked us
out. It was the monstrous swift shadow cone of the moon. I have since
read that this wave of shadow moves 1,800 miles an hour. Language
can give no sense of this sort of speed—1,800 miles an hour. It was 195
miles wide. No end was in sight—you saw only the edge. It rolled at
you across the land at 1,800 miles an hour, hauling darkness like
plague behind it. Seeing it, and knowing it was coming straight for
you, was like feeling a slug of anesthetic shoot up your arm. If you
think very fast, you may have time to think, "Soon it will hit my brain."
You can feel the deadness race up your arm; you can feel the ap-
palling, inhuman speed of your own blood. We saw the wall of shadow
coming, and screamed before it hit.

    This was the universe about which we have read so much and never   48
before felt: the universe as a clockwork of loose spheres flung at stupe-
fying, unauthorized speeds. How could anything moving so fast not
crash, not veer from its orbit amok like a car out of control on a turn?

    Less than two minutes later, when the sun emerged, the trailing   49
edge of the shadow cone sped away. It coursed down our hill and
raced eastward over the plain, faster than the eye could believe; it
swept over the plain and dropped over the planet's rim in a twinkling.
It had clobbered us, and now it roared away. We blinked in the light. It
was as though an enormous, loping god in the sky had reached down
and slapped the earth's face.

    Something else, something more ordinary, came back to me along   50
about the third cup of coffee. During the moments of totality, it was so

dark that drivers on the highway below turned on their cars' headlights. We could see the highway's route as a strand of lights. It was
bumper-to-bumper down there. It was eight-fifteen in the morning,
Monday morning, and people were driving into Yakima to work. That
it was as dark as night, and eerie as hell, an hour after dawn, apparently meant that in order to *see* to drive to work, people had to use
their headlights. Four or five cars pulled off the road. The rest, in a line
at least five miles long, drove to town. The highway ran between hills;
the people could not have seen any of the eclipsed sun at all. Yakima
will have another total eclipse in 2086. Perhaps, in 2086, businesses
will give their employees an hour off.

From the restaurant we drove back to the coast. The highway cross-   51
ing the Cascades range was open. We drove over the mountain like old
pros. We joined our places on the planet's thin crust; it held. For the
time being, we were home free.

Early that morning at six, when we had checked out, the six bald   52
men were sitting on folding chairs in the dim hotel lobby. The television was on. Most of them were awake. You might drown in your own
spittle, God knows, at any time; you might wake up dead in a small
hotel, a cabbage head watching TV while snows pile up in the passes,
watching TV while the chili peppers smile and the moon passes over
the sun and nothing changes and nothing is learned because you
have lost your bucket and shovel and no longer care. What if you
regain the surface and open your sack and find, instead of treasure,
a beast which jumps at you? Or you may not come back at all. The
winches may jam, the scaffolding buckle, the air conditioning collapse. You may glance up one day and see by your headlamp the
canary keeled over in its cage. You may reach into a cranny for pearls
and touch a moray eel. You yank on your rope; it is too late.

Apparently people share a sense of these hazards, for when the   53
total eclipse ended, an odd thing happened.

When the sun appeared as a blinding bead on the ring's side, the   54
eclipse was over. The black lens cover appeared again, backlighted,
and slid away. At once the yellow light made the sky blue again;
the black lid dissolved and vanished. The real world began there. I
remember now: we all hurried away. We were born and bored at a
stroke. We rushed down the hill. We found our car; we saw the other
people streaming down the hillsides; we joined the highway traffic
and drove away.

We never looked back. It was a general vamoose, and an odd one,   55
for when we left the hill, the sun was still partially eclipsed—a sight
rare enough, and one which, in itself, we would probably have driven
five hours to see. But enough is enough. One turns at last even from

glory itself with a sigh of relief. From the depths of mystery, and even from the heights of splendor, we bounce back and hurry for the latitudes of home.

QUESTIONS FOR DISCUSSION

1   What feelings does the image of the "lifelike painting of a smiling clown's head, made out of vegetables," evoke in Dillard and in you, the reader? How does she use this image as a stepping-stone for developing her thoughts about the meaning of the total eclipse?

2   Why does Dillard claim that in the case of the total eclipse, "What you see is more convincing than any wild-eyed theory you may know?" How does the eclipse affect her understanding of the relationship between theories of the natural world and the experience of the natural world?

3   How does Dillard's image of herself "standing in a movie of hillside grasses filmed in the Middle Ages" capture her sense of dislocation during the eclipse? Why does she feel that she is dead? How did you respond to her "vision"?

4   Why are the people who are witnessing the eclipse screaming? What is most frightening to you about the eclipse as Dillard describes it?

5   As the eclipse ends, Dillard contrasts the emerging ring of light around the sun to an old silver wedding band or a morsel of bone. What meaning does she imply by each image? What is the impact of these sharply contrasting images?

IDEAS FOR WRITING

1   Write about an inspiring natural event, such as a total eclipse, that you experienced or witnessed with other people. Discuss the psychological and spiritual effect that the event had on you as an individual and on your community.

2   Write an essay that interprets the spiritual meanings in Dillard's account of the total eclipse.

Nature and the Scientific Mind

Evolution as Fact and Theory

STEPHEN JAY GOULD

Stephen Jay Gould (b. 1941), an evolutionary biologist and a paleontologist, is a widely read writer who makes difficult scientific concepts understandable and exciting. Gould often writes about the unexpected within nature because he believes that natural history is significantly altered by events that are out of the ordinary. Born and raised in New York City, Gould completed his A.B. at Antioch College in 1963 and his Ph.D. at Columbia University in 1967. He has been teaching at Harvard University since the late 1960s. He writes a regular column, "This View of Life," for Natural History Magazine. *Many of his columns are included in essay collections. Some of his most widely read collections are* Ever Since Darwin *(1977),* The Panda's Thumb *(1980),* Hen's Teeth and Horse's Toes *(1983),* The Flamingo's Smile *(1985), and* Dinosaur in a Haystack *(1996).*

Kirtley Mather, who died last year [1978] at age 89, was a pillar of both science and the Christian religion in America and one of my dearest friends. The difference of half a century in our ages evaporated before our common interests. The most curious thing we shared was a battle we each fought at the same age. For Kirtley had gone to Tennessee with Clarence Darrow to testify for evolution at the Scopes trial of 1925. When I think that we are enmeshed again in the same struggle for one of the best documented, most compelling and exciting concepts in all science, I don't know whether to laugh or cry.   1

According to idealized principles of scientific discourse, the arousal of dormant issues should reflect fresh data that give renewed life to abandoned notions. Those outside the current debate may therefore be excused for suspecting that creationists have come up with something new, or that evolutionists have generated some serious internal trouble. But nothing has changed; the creationists have not a single new fact or argument. Darrow and Bryan were at least more entertaining than we lesser antagonists today.* The rise of creationism is politics, pure and simple; it represents one issue (and by no means the major concern) of the resurgent evangelical right. Arguments that seemed kooky just a decade ago have re-entered the mainstream.   2

---

*Darrow and Bryan: Clarence Darrow (1857–1938) was the defense attorney in the 1925 trial of John Thomas Scopes for teaching evolution; William Jennings Bryan (1860–1925) was an orator and politician who aided the prosecution in the Scopes trial. [Eds.]

Creationism Is Not Science

The basic attack of the creationists falls apart on two general counts   3
before we even reach the supposed factual details of their complaints
against evolution. First, they play upon a vernacular misunderstand-
ing of the word "theory" to convey the false impression that we evolutionists are covering up the rotten core of our edifice. Second, they
misuse a popular philosophy of science to argue that they are be-
having scientifically in attacking evolution. Yet the same philosophy
demonstrates that their own belief is not science, and that "scientific
creationism" is therefore meaningless and self-contradictory, a superb
example of what Orwell† called "newspeak."‡

In the American vernacular, "theory" often means "imperfect   4
fact"—part of a hierarchy of confidence running downhill from fact to
theory to hypothesis to guess. Thus the power of the creationist argument: evolution is "only" a theory, and intense debate now rages
about many aspects of the theory. If evolution is less than a fact, and
scientists can't even make up their minds about the theory, then what
confidence can we have in it? Indeed, President Reagan echoed this
argument before an evangelical group in Dallas when he said (in what
I devoutly hope was campaign rhetoric): "Well, it is a theory. It is a
scientific theory only, and it has in recent years been challenged in the
world of science—that is, not believed in the scientific community to
be as infallible as it once was."

Well, evolution *is* a theory. It is also a fact. And facts and theories   5
are different things, not rungs in a hierarchy of increasing certainty.
Facts are the world's data. Theories are structures of ideas that explain
and interpret facts. Facts do not go away when scientists debate rival
theories to explain them. Einstein's theory of gravitation replaced
Newton's, but apples did not suspend themselves in mid-air pending
the outcome. And human beings evolved from apelike ancestors
whether they did so by Darwin's proposed mechanism or by some
other, yet to be discovered.

Moreover, "fact" does not mean "absolute certainty." The final   6
proofs of logic and mathematics flow deductively from stated
premises and achieve certainty only because they are *not* about
the empirical world. Evolutionists make no claim for perpetual
truth, though creationists often do (and then attack us for a style of
argument that they themselves favor). In science, "fact" can only
mean "confirmed to such a degree that it would be perverse to with-
hold provisional assent." I suppose that apples might start to rise

†George Orwell (1903–1950): English journalist and novelist, author of *Animal Farm*
and *1984*. [Eds.]
‡"Newspeak": the official language in Orwell's *1984*, devised to meet the ideological
needs of the ruling party and to make all other modes of thought impossible. [Eds.]

tomorrow, but the possibility does not merit equal time to physics classrooms.

Evolutionists have been clear about this distinction between fact   7
and theory from the very beginning, if only because we have always acknowledged how far we are from completely understanding the mechanisms (theory) by which evolution (fact) occurred. Darwin continually emphasized the difference between his two great and separate accomplishments: establishing the fact of evolution, and proposing a theory—natural selection—to explain the mechanism of evolution. He wrote in *The Descent of Man:* "I had two distinct objects in view; firstly, to show that species had not been separately created, and secondly, that natural selection had been the chief agent of change. . . . Hence if I have erred in . . . having exaggerated its [natural selection's] power . . . I have at least, as I hope, done good service in aiding to overthrow the dogma of separate creations."

Thus Darwin acknowledged the provisional nature of natural selec-   8
tion while affirming the fact of evolution. The fruitful theoretical de-
bate that Darwin initiated has never ceased. From the 1940s through the 1960s, Darwin's own theory of natural selection did achieve a temporary hegemony that it never enjoyed in his lifetime. But renewed debate characterizes our decade, and, while no biologist questions the importance of natural selection, many now doubt its ubiquity. In particular, many evolutionists argue that substantial amounts of genetic change may not be subject to natural selection and may spread through populations at random. Others are challenging Darwin's linking of natural selection with gradual, imperceptible change through all intermediary degrees; they are arguing that most evolutionary events may occur far more rapidly than Darwin envisioned.

Scientists regard debates on fundamental issues of theory as a sign   9
of intellectual health and a source of excitement. Science is—and how else can I say it?—most fun when it plays with interesting ideas, examines their implications, and recognizes that old information may be explained in surprisingly new ways. Evolutionary theory is now en-
joying this uncommon vigor. Yet amidst all this turmoil no biologist has been led to doubt the fact that evolution occurred; we are debat-
ing *how* it happened. We are all trying to explain the same thing: the tree of evolutionary descent linking all organisms by ties of genealogy. Creationists pervert and caricature this debate by conveniently neglecting the common conviction that underlies it, and by falsely suggesting that we now doubt the very phenomenon we are strug-
gling to understand.

Using another invalid argument, creationists claim that "the dogma   10
of separate creations," as Darwin characterized it a century ago, is a scientific theory meriting equal time with evolution in high school biology curricula. But a prevailing viewpoint among philosophers of

science belies this creationist argument. Philosopher Karl Popper has argued for decades that the primary criterion of science is the falsifiability of its theories. We can never prove absolutely, but we can falsify. A set of ideas that cannot, in principle, be falsified is not science.

The entire creationist argument involves little more than a rhetorical attempt to falsify evolution by presenting supposed contradictions among its supporters. Their brand of creationism, they claim, is "scientific" because it follows the Popperian model in trying to demolish evolution. Yet Popper's argument must apply in both directions. One does not become a scientist by the simple act of trying to falsify another scientific system; one has to present an alternative system that also meets Popper's criterion—it too must be falsifiable in principle.   11

"Scientific creationism" is a self-contradictory, nonsense phrase precisely because it cannot be falsified. I can envision observations and experiments that would disapprove any evolutionary theory I know, but I cannot imagine what potential data could lead creationists to abandon their beliefs. Unbeatable systems are dogma, not science. Lest I seem harsh or rhetorical, I quote creationism's leading intellectual, Duane Gish, Ph.D., from his recent (1978) book *Evolution? The Fossils Say No!* "By creation we mean the bringing into being by a supernatural Creator of the basic kinds of plants and animals by the process of sudden, or fiat, creation. We do not know how the Creator created, what processes He used, *for He used processes which are not now operating anywhere in the natural universe* [Gish's italics]. This is why we refer to creation as special creation. We cannot discover by scientific investigations anything about the creative processes used by the Creator." Pray tell, Dr. Gish, in the light of your last sentence, what then is "scientific" creationism?   12

The Fact of Evolution

Our confidence that evolution occurred centers upon three general arguments. First, we have abundant, direct, observational evidence of evolution in action, from both the field and the laboratory. It ranges from countless experiments on change in nearly everything about fruit flies subjected to artificial selection in the laboratory to the famous British moths that turned black when industrial soot darkened the trees upon which they rest. (The moths gain protection from sharp-sighted bird predators by blending into the background.) Creationists do not deny these observations; how could they? Creationists have tightened their act. They now argue that God only created "basic kinds," and allowed for limited evolutionary meandering within them. Thus toy poodles and Great Danes come from the dog kind and moths can change color, but nature cannot convert a dog to a cat or a monkey to a man.   13

The second and third arguments for evolution—the case for major   14
changes—do not involve direct observation of evolution in action.
They rest upon inference, but are no less secure for that reason. Major
evolutionary change requires too much time for direct observation on
the scale of recorded human history. All historical sciences rest upon
inference, and evolution is no different from geology, cosmology, or
human history in this respect. In principle, we cannot observe
processes that operated in the past. We must infer them from results
that still survive: living and fossil organisms for evolution, documents
and artifacts for human history, strata and topography for geology.

The second argument—that the imperfection of nature reveals evo-   15
lution—strikes many people as ironic, for they feel that evolution
should be most elegantly displayed in the nearly perfect adaptation expressed by some organisms—the chamber of a gull's wing, or butterflies that cannot be seen in ground litter because they mimic leaves so
precisely. But perfection could be imposed by a wise creator or evolved
by natural selection. Perfection covers the tracks of past history. And
past history—the evidence of descent—is our mark of evolution.

Evolution lies exposed in the *imperfections* that record a history of   16
descent. Why should a rat run, a bat fly, a porpoise swim, and I type
this essay with structures built of the same bones unless we all inherited them from a common ancestor? An engineer, starting from
scratch, could design better limbs in each case. Why should all the
large native mammals of Australia be marsupials, unless they descended from a common ancestor isolated on this island continent?
Marsupials are not "better," or ideally suited for Australia; many have
been wiped out by placental mammals imported by man from other
continents. This principle of imperfection extends to all historical
sciences. When we recognize the etymology of September, October,
November, and December (seventh, eighth, ninth, and tenth, from
the Latin), we know that two additional items (January and February)
must have been added to an original calendar of ten months.

The third argument is more direct: transitions are often found in the   17
fossil record. Preserved transitions are not common—and should not
be, according to our understanding of evolution . . . —but they are not
entirely wanting, as creationists often claim. The lower jaw of reptiles
contains several bones, that of mammals only one. The nonmam-   .
malian jawbones are reduced, step by step, in mammalian ancestors
until they become tiny nubbins located at the back of the jaw. The
"hammer" and "anvil" bones of the mammalian ear are descendants of
these nubbins. How could such a transition be accomplished? the
creationists ask. Surely a bone is entirely in the jaw or in the ear. Yet
paleontologists have discovered two transitional lineages or therap-
sids (the so-called mammal-like reptiles) with a double jaw joint—one
composed of the old quadrate and articular bones (soon to become
the hammer and anvil), the other of the squamosal and dentary bones

(as in modern mammals). For that matter, what better transitional form could we desire than the oldest human, *Australopithecus afarensis,* with its apelike palate, its human upright stance, and a cranial capacity larger than any ape's of the same body size but a full 1,000 cubic centimeters below ours? If God made each of the half dozen human species discovered in ancient rocks, why did he create an unbroken temporal sequence of progressively more modern features—increasing cranial capacity, reduced face and teeth, larger body size? Did he create to mimic evolution and test our faith thereby? . . .

Conclusion

I am both angry at and amused by the creationists; but mostly I am deeply sad. Sad for many reasons. Sad because so many people who respond to creationist appeals are troubled for the right reason, but venting their anger at the wrong target. It is true that scientists have often been dogmatic and elitist. It is true that we have often allowed the white-coated, advertising image to represent us—"Scientists say that Brand X cures bunions ten times faster than. . . ." We have not fought it adequately because we derive benefits from appearing as a new priesthood. It is also true that faceless bureaucratic state power intrudes more and more into our lives and removes choices that should belong to individuals and communities. I can understand that requiring that evolution be taught in the schools might be seen as one more insult on all these grounds. But the culprit is not, and cannot be, evolution or any other fact of the natural world. Identify and fight your legitimate enemies by all means, but we are not among them.   18

I am sad because the practical result of this brouhaha will not be expanded coverage to include creationism (that would also make me sad), but the reduction or excision of evolution from high school curricula. Evolution is one of the half dozen "great ideas" developed by science. It speaks to the profound issues of genealogy that fascinate all of us—the "roots" phenomenon writ large. Where did we come from? Where did life arise? How did it develop? How are organisms related? It forces us to think, ponder, and wonder. Shall we deprive millions of this knowledge and once again teach biology as a set of dull and unconnected facts, without the thread that weaves diverse material into a supple unity?   19

But most of all I am saddened by a trend I am just beginning to discern among my colleagues. I sense that some now wish to mute the healthy debate about theory that has brought new life to evolutionary biology. It provides grist for creationist mills, they say, even if only by distortion. Perhaps we should lie low and rally round the flag of strict Darwinism, at least for the moment—a kind of old-time religion on our part.   20

But we should borrow another metaphor and recognize that we too   21
have to tread a straight and narrow path, surrounded by roads to
perdition. For if we ever begin to suppress our search to understand
nature, to quench our own intellectual excitement in a misguided
effort to present a united front where it does not and should not exist,
then we are truly lost.

QUESTIONS FOR DISCUSSION

1   How do the first two paragraphs establish Gould's point of view?
    How does Gould attempt to capture the reader's interest?

2   How does Gould explain the scientific concept of theory, and how
    does he refute the creationists' attempts to reduce evolution to
    just a "theory"?

3   Why is Gould critical of the creationists' attempts to discredit the
    theory of evolution and to change the way biology is taught in
    high school?

4   Do you think that Darwin's explanation of the mechanism of evo-
    lution allows for the possibility of a divine being? Can common
    ground be found between evolutionary ideas and Western reli-
    gious concepts of God and creation? Explain your point of view.

5   What three arguments does Gould propose in support of evolu-
    tion? How does he use observed facts and details to support his
    point of view?

IDEAS FOR WRITING

1   Explain in an essay why you agree or disagree with the theory of
    evolution. Use examples from your own background knowledge,
    as well as current theory, to support your perspective.

2   Write a response to Gould's argument against creationism.

Learning to See

FARLEY MOWAT

One of Canada's most highly respected and best-loved nature writers, Farley Mowat was born in Belleville, Ontario, in 1921. He spent much time during his childhood traveling throughout Canada with his family and their many pets. After serving in the Canadian Army during World War II, Mowat moved to the Canadian Arctic. His writing expresses deep sympathy for threatened species and cultures. Some of his more widely read works are A Whale for the Killing *(1972),* The Snow Walker *(1975),* Sea of Slaughter *(1984),* Woman in the Mists: The Story of Dian Fossey and the Mountain Gorillas of Africa *(1987), and* Rescue the Earth *(1990). The selection that follows is from* Never Cry Wolf *(1963), an account of his adventures as a field biologist in the Arctic, which was made into a movie in 1983.*

1   The lack of sustained interest which the big male wolf had displayed toward me was encouraging enough to tempt me to visit the den again the next morning; but this time, instead of the shotgun and the hatchet (I still retained the rifle, pistol and hunting knife) I carried a high-powered periscopic telescope and a tripod on which to mount it.

2   It was a fine sunny morning with enough breeze to keep the mosquito vanguard down. When I reached the bay where the esker was, I chose a prominent knoll of rock some four hundred yards from the den, behind which I could set up my telescope so that its objective lenses peered over the crest, but left me in hiding. Using consummate fieldcraft, I approached the chosen observation point in such a manner that the wolves could not possibly have seen me and, since the wind was from them to me, I assured that they would have had no suspicion of my arrival.

3   When all was in order, I focused the telescope; but to my chagrin I could see no wolves. The magnification of the instrument was such that I could almost distinguish the individual grains of sand in the esker; yet, though I searched every inch of it for a distance of a mile on each side of the den, I could find no indication that wolves were about, or had ever been about. By noon, I had a bad case of eyestrain and a worse one of cramps, and I had almost concluded that my hypothesis of the previous day was grievously at fault and that the "den" was just a fortuitous hole in the sand.

4   This was discouraging, for it had begun to dawn on me that all of the intricate study plans and schedules which I had drawn up were not going to be of much use without a great deal of co-operation on the part of the wolves. In country as open and as vast as this one was,

the prospects of getting within visual range of a wolf except by the luckiest of accidents (and I had already had more than my ration of these) were negligible. I realized that if this was not a wolves' den which I had found, I had about as much chance of locating the actual den in this faceless wilderness as I had of finding a diamond mine.

Glumly I went back to my unproductive survey through the tele-   5
scope. The esker remained deserted. The hot sand began sending up heat waves which increased by eyestrain. By 2:00 P.M. I had given up hope. There seemed no further point in concealment, so I got stiffly to my feet and prepared to relieve myself.

Now it is a remarkable fact that a man, even though he may be   6
alone in a small boat in mid-ocean, or isolated in the midst of the trackless forest, finds that the very process of unbuttoning causes him to become peculiarly sensitive to the possibility that he may be under observation. At this critical juncture none but the most self-assured of men, no matter how certain he may be of his privacy, can refrain from casting a surreptitious glance around to reassure himself that he really is alone.

To say I was chagrined to discover I was *not* alone would be an   7
understatement; for sitting directly behind me, and not twenty yards away, were the missing wolves.

They appeared to be quite relaxed and comfortable, as if they had   8
been sitting there behind my back for hours. The big male seemed a trifle bored; but the female's gaze was fixed on me with what I took to be an expression of unabashed and even prurient curiosity.

The human psyche is truly an amazing thing. Under almost any   9
other circumstances I would probably have been panic-stricken, and I think few would have blamed me for it. But these were not ordinary circumstances and my reaction was one of violent indignation. Outraged, I turned my back on the watching wolves and with fingers which were shaking with vexation, hurriedly did up my buttons. When decency, if not my dignity, had been restored, I rounded on those wolves with a virulence which surprised even me.

"Shoo!" I screamed at them. "What the hell do you think you're at,   10
you . . . you . . . peeping Toms! Go away, for heaven's sake!"

The wolves were startled. They sprang to their feet, glanced at   11
each other with a wild surmise, and then trotted off, passed down a draw, and disappeared in the direction of the esker. They did not once look back.

With their departure I experienced a reaction of another kind. The   12
realization that they had been sitting almost within jumping distance of my unprotected back for God knows how long set up such a turmoil of the spirit that I had to give up all thought of carrying on where my discovery of the wolves had forced me to leave off. Suffering from

both mental and physical strain, therefore, I hurriedly packed my gear and set out for the cabin.

My thoughts that evening were confused. True, my prayer had been answered, and the wolves had certainly co-operated by reappearing; but on the other hand I was becoming prey to a small but nagging doubt as to just *who* was watching *whom*. I felt that I, because of my specific superiority as a member of *Homo sapiens,* together with my intensive technical training, was entitled to pride of place. The sneaking suspicion that this pride had been denied and that, in point of fact, *I* was the one who was under observation, had an unsettling effect upon my ego.   13

In order to establish my ascendancy once and for all, I determined to visit the wolf esker itself the following morning and make a detailed examination of the presumed den. I decided to go by canoe, since the rivers were now clear and the rafting lake ice was being driven off-shore by a stiff northerly breeze.   14

It was a fine, leisurely trip to Wolf House Bay, as I had now named it. The annual spring caribou migration north from the forested areas of Manitoba toward the distant tundra plains near Dubawnt Lake was under way, and from my canoe I could see countless skeins of caribou crisscrossing the muskegs and the rolling hills in all directions. No wolves were in evidence as I neared the esker, and I assumed they were away hunting a caribou for lunch.   15

I ran the canoe ashore and, fearfully laden with cameras, guns, binoculars and other gear, laboriously climbed the shifting sands of the esker to the shadowy place where the female wolf had disappeared. En route I found unmistakable proof that this esker was, if not the home, at least one of the favorite promenades of the wolves. It was liberally strewn with scats and covered with wolf tracks which in many places formed well-defined paths.   16

The den was located in a small wadi in the esker, and was so well concealed that I was on the point of walking past without seeing it, when a series of small squeaks attracted my attention. I stopped and turned to look, and there, not fifteen feet below me, were four small, gray beasties engaged in a free-for-all wrestling match.   17

At first I did not recognize them for what they were. The fat, fox faces with pinprick ears; the butterball bodies, as round as pumpkins; the short, bowed legs and the tiny upthrust sprigs of tails were so far from my conception of a wolf that my brain refused to make the logical connection.   18

Suddenly one of the pups caught my scent. He stopped in the midst of attempting to bite off a brother's tail and turned smoky blue eyes up toward me. What he saw evidently intrigued him. Lurching free of the scrimmage, he padded toward me with a rolling, wobbly gait; but   19 a flea bit him unexpectedly before he had gone far, and he had to sit down to scratch it.

At this instant an adult wolf let loose a full-throated howl vibrant with alarm and warning, not more than fifty yards from me.   20

The idyllic scene exploded into frenzied action.   21

The pups became gray streaks which vanished into the gaping darkness of the den mouth. I spun around to face the adult wolf, lost my footing, and started to skid down the loose slope toward the den. In trying to regain my balance I thrust the muzzle of the rifle deep into the sand, where it stuck fast until the carrying-strap dragged it free as I slid rapidly away from it. I fumbled wildly at my revolver, but so cluttered was I with cameras and equipment straps that I did not succeed in getting the weapon clear as, accompanied by a growing avalanche of sand, I shot past the den mouth, over the lip of the main ridge and down the full length of the esker slope. Miraculously, I kept my feet; but only by dint of superhuman contortions during which I was alternately bent forward like a skier going over a jump, or leaning backward at such an acute angle I thought my backbone was going to snap.   22

It must have been quite a show. When I got myself straightened out and glanced back up the esker, it was to see *three* adult wolves ranged side by side like spectators in the Royal Box, all peering down at me with expressions of incredulous delight.   23

I lost my temper. This is something a scientist seldom does, but I lost mine. My dignity had been too heavily eroded during the past several days and my scientific detachment was no longer equal to the strain. With a snarl of exasperation I raised the rifle but, fortunately, the thing was so clogged with sand that when I pressed the trigger nothing happened.   24

The wolves did not appear alarmed until they saw me begin to dance up and down in helpless fury, waving the useless rifle and hurling imprecations at their cocked ears; whereupon they exchanged quizzical looks and silently withdrew out of my sight.   25

I too withdrew, for I was in no fit mental state to carry on with my exacting scientific duties. To tell the truth, I was in no fit mental state to do anything except hurry home to Mike's and seek solace for my tattered nerves and frayed vanity in the bottom of a jar of wolf-juice.   26

I had a long and salutary session with the stuff that night, and as my spiritual bruises became less painful under its healing influence, I reviewed the incidents of the past few days. Inescapably, the realization was being borne in upon my preconditioned mind that the centuries-old and universally accepted human concept of wolf character was a palpable lie. On three separate occasions in less than a week I had been completely at the mercy of these "savage killers"; but far from attempting to tear me limb from limb, they had displayed a restraint verging on contempt, even when I invaded their home and appeared to be posing a direct threat to the young pups.   27

This much was obvious, yet I was still strangely reluctant to let the   28
myth go down the drain. Part of this reluctance was no doubt due to
the thought that, by discarding the accepted concepts of wolf nature,
I would be committing scientific treason; part of it to the knowledge
that recognition of the truth would deprive my mission of its fine aura
of danger and high adventure; and not the least part of that reluctance
was probably due to my unwillingness to accept the fact that I had
been made to look like a blithering idiot—not by my fellow man, but
by mere brute beasts.

Nevertheless I persevered.   29

When I emerged from my session with the wolf-juice the following   30
morning I was somewhat the worse for wear in a physical sense; but I
was cleansed and purified spiritually. I had wrestled with my devils
and I had won. I had made my decision that, from this hour onward,
I would go open-minded into the lupine world and learn to see and
know the wolves, not for what they were supposed to be, but for what
the actually were.

QUESTIONS FOR DISCUSSION

1   How does Mowat discover the wolves? What range of feelings does
    he experience once he realizes that they have been watching him?
2   What role does Mowat's scientific knowledge play in his under-
    standing and study of the wolves?
3   How does Mowat characterize himself? Is he an able and objec-
    tive scientist? Explain.
4   Why is Mowat reluctant to stop believing in the myth of the wolf
    as "savage killer" even after he has had three encounters with
    wolves who have behaved with restraint?
5   How does Mowat explain his spiritual cleansing? Do you think
    that his study of the wolves will be successful? Explain your point
    of view.

IDEAS FOR WRITING

1   Write an essay about an encounter that you have had with un-
    familiar animals. What myths about the animals did you believe
    before your encounter? In what ways were your attitudes changed
    as a result?
2   Write a paper that explores some of the reasons that people have
    been interested in understanding animals in their natural set-
    tings. You may want to focus on the motivations of an individual,
    such as Farley Mowat or Dian Fossey (see her essay in the next
    section of this book).

The Clan of One-Breasted Women

TERRY TEMPEST WILLIAMS

*Terry Tempest Williams (b. 1959) was raised in Nevada and
attended the Teton Science School where she earned a B.A. in
English and an M.A. in environmental education. She now works
as a naturalist for the Utah Museum of Natural History and lives
with her husband in the mountains outside Salt Lake City. Her style
is intense and lyrical; her works often imply that women can be the
best intermediaries or interpreters of the relationships between the
natural world and human conduct. Her most widely read works are*
Pieces of White Shell *(1984),* Coyote's Canyon *(1989),* An Unspoken
Hunger *(1994), and* Desert Quartet *(1995). Her latest work is* A Love
That Is Wild *(Random House, 1998). The following selection, "The
Clan of One-Breasted Women," excerpted from* Refuge: An Unnatural
History of Family and Place *(1991), asks us to face the serious long-
term consequences of nuclear testing.*

I belong to a Clan of One-Breasted Women. My mother, my grand-   1
mothers, and six aunts have all had mastectomies. Seven are dead.
The two who survive have just completed rounds of chemotherapy
and radiation.

I've had my own problems: two biopsies for breast cancer and a   2
small tumor between my ribs diagnosed as a "borderline malignancy."

This is my family history.   3

Most statistics tell us breast cancer is genetic, hereditary, with ris-   4
ing percentages attached to fatty diets, childlessness, or becoming
pregnant after thirty. What they don't say is living in Utah may be the
greatest hazard of all.

We are a Mormon family with roots in Utah since 1847. The "word of   5
wisdom" in my family aligned us with good foods—no coffee, no tea,
tobacco, or alcohol. For the most part, our women were finished having their babies by the time they were thirty. And only one faced breast
cancer prior to 1960. Traditionally, as a group of people, Mormons
have a low rate of cancer.

Is our family a cultural anomaly? The truth is, we didn't think about   6
it. Those who did, usually the men, simply said, "bad genes." The
women's attitude was stoic. Cancer was part of life. On February 16,
1971, the eve of my mother's surgery, I accidently picked up the tele-
phone and overheard her ask my grandmother what she could expect.

"Diane, it is one of the most spiritual experiences you will ever   7
encounter."

I quietly put down the receiver.   8

Two days later, my father took my brothers and me to the hospital   9
to visit her. She met us in the lobby in a wheelchair. No bandages were
visible. I'll never forget her radiance, the way she held herself in a
purple velvet robe, and how she gathered us around her.

"Children, I am fine. I want you to know I felt the arms of God   10
around me."

We believed her. My father cried. Our mother, his wife, was thirty-   11
eight years old.

A little over a year after Mother's death, Dad and I were having dinner   12
together. He had just returned from St. George, where the Tempest
Company was completing the gas lines that would service southern
Utah. He spoke of his love for the country, the sandstoned landscape,
bare-boned and beautiful. He had just finished hiking the Kolob trail
in Zion National Park. We got caught up in reminiscing, recalling with
fondness our walk up Angel's Landing on his fiftieth birthday and the
years our family had vacationed there.

Over dessert, I shared a recurring dream of mine. I told my father   13
that for years, as long as I could remember, I saw this flash of light in
the night in the desert—that this image had so permeated my being
that I could not venture south without seeing it again, on the horizon,
illuminating buttes and mesas.

"You did see it," he said.   14

"Saw what?"   15

"The bomb. The cloud. We were driving home from Riverside, Cali-   16
fornia. You were sitting on Diane's lap. She was pregnant. In fact, I
remember the day, September 7, 1957. We had just gotten out of the
Service. We were driving north, past Las Vegas. It was an hour or so
before dawn, when this explosion went off. We not only heard it, but
felt it. I thought the oil tanker in front of us had blown up. We pulled
over and suddenly, rising from the desert floor, we saw it, clearly, this
golden-stemmed cloud, the mushroom. The sky seemed to vibrate
with an eerie pink glow. Within a few minutes, a light ash was raining
on the car."

I stared at my father.   17

"I thought you knew that," he said. "It was a common occurrence   18
in the fifties."

It was at this moment that I realized the deceit I had been living   19
under. Children growing up in the American Southwest, drinking
contaminated milk from contaminated cows, even from the contaminated breasts of their mothers, my mother—members, years later, of
the Clan of One-Breasted Women.

It is a well-known story in the Desert West, "The Day We Bombed   20
Utah," or more accurately, the years we bombed Utah: above ground
atomic testing in Nevada took place from January 27, 1951 through
July 11, 1962. Not only were the winds blowing north covering "low-use

segments of the population" with fallout and leaving sheep dead in their tracks, but the climate was right. The United States of the 1950s was red, white, and blue. The Korean War was raging. McCarthyism was rampant. Ike was it, and the cold war was hot. If you were against nuclear testing, you were for a communist regime.

Much has been written about this "American nuclear tragedy." 21 Public health was secondary to national security. The Atomic Energy Commissioner, Thomas Murray, said, "Gentlemen, we must not let anything interfere with this series of tests, nothing."

Again and again, the American public was told by its government, 22 in spite of burns, blisters, and nausea, "It has been found that the tests may be conducted with adequate assurance of safety under conditions prevailing at the bombing reservations." Assuaging public fears was simply a matter of public relations. "Your best action," an Atomic Energy Commission booklet read, "is not to be worried about fallout." A news release typical of the times stated, "We find no basis for concluding that harm to any individual has resulted from radio-active fallout."

On August 30, 1979, during Jimmy Carter's presidency, a suit was 23 filed, *Irene Allen v. The United States of America*. Mrs. Allen's case was the first on an alphabetical list of twenty-four test cases, repre-sentative of nearly twelve hundred plaintiffs seeking compensation from the United States government for cancers caused by nuclear testing in Nevada.

Irene Allen lived in Hurricane, Utah. She was the mother of five 24 children and had been widowed twice. Her first husband, with their two oldest boys, had watched the tests from the roof of the local high school. He died of leukemia in 1956. Her second husband died of pancreatic cancer in 1978.

In a town meeting conducted by Utah Senator Orrin Hatch, shortly 25 before the suit was filed, Mrs. Allen said, "I am not blaming the gov-ernment, I want you to know that, Senator Hatch. But I thought if my testimony could help in any way so this wouldn't happen again to any of the generations coming up after us . . . I am happy to be here this day to bear testimony of this."

God-fearing people. This is just one story in an anthology of 26 thousands.

On May 10, 1984, Judge Bruce S. Jenkins handed down his opinion. 27 Ten of the plaintiffs were awarded damages. It was the first time a fed-eral court had determined that nuclear tests had been the cause of cancers. For the remaining fourteen test cases, the proof of causation was not sufficient. In spite of the split decision, it was considered a landmark ruling. It was not to remain so for long.

In April 1987, the Tenth Circuit Court of Appeals overturned Judge 28 Jenkins's ruling on the ground that the United States was protected from suit by the legal doctrine of sovereign immunity, a centuries-old idea from England in the days of absolute monarchs.

In January 1988, the Supreme Court refused to review the Appeals Court decision. To our court system it does not matter whether the United States government was irresponsible, whether it lied to its citizens, or even that citizens died from the fallout of nuclear testing. What matters is that our government is immune: "The King can do no wrong." 29

In Mormon culture, authority is respected, obedience is revered, and independent thinking is not. I was taught as a young girl not to "make waves" or "rock the boat." 30

"Just let it go," Mother would say. "You know how you feel, that's what counts." 31

For many years, I have done just that—listened, observed, and quietly formed my own opinions, in a culture that rarely asks questions because it has all the answers. But one by one, I have watched the women in my family die common, heroic deaths. We sat in waiting rooms hoping for good news, but always receiving the bad. I cared for them, bathed their scarred bodies, and kept their secrets. I watched beautiful women become bald as Cytoxan, cisplatin, and Adriamycin were injected into their veins. I held their foreheads as they vomited green-black bile, and I shot them with morphine when the pain became inhuman. In the end, I witnessed their last peaceful breaths, becoming a midwife to the rebirth of their souls. 32

The price of obedience has become too high. 33

The fear and inability to question authority that ultimately killed rural communities in Utah during atmospheric testing of atomic weapons is the same fear I saw in my mother's body. Sheep. Dead sheep. The evidence is buried. 34

I cannot prove that my mother, Diane Dixon Tempest, or my grandmothers, Lettie Romney Dixon and Kathryn Blackett Tempest, along with my aunts developed cancer from nuclear fallout in Utah. But I can't prove they didn't. 35

My father's memory was correct. The September blast we drove through in 1957 was part of Operation Plumbbob, one of the most intensive series of bomb tests to be initiated. The flash of light in the night in the desert, which I had always thought was a dream, developed into a family nightmare. It took fourteen years, from 1957 to 1971, for cancer to manifest in my mother—the same time, Howard L. Andrews, an authority in radioactive fallout at the National Institutes of Health, says radiation cancer requires to become evident. The more I learn about what it means to be a "downwinder," the more questions I drown in. 36

What I do know, however, is that as a Mormon woman of the fifth generation of Latter-day Saints, I must question everything, even if 37 it means losing my faith, even if it means becoming a member of a border tribe among my own people. Tolerating blind obedience in the name of patriotism or religion ultimately takes our lives.

When the Atomic Energy Commission described the country north   38
of the Nevada Test Site as "virtually uninhabited desert terrain," my family and the birds at Great Salt Lake were some of the "virtual uninhabitants."

One night, I dreamed women from all over the world circled a blaz-   39
ing fire in the desert. They spoke of change, how they hold the moon in their bellies and wax and wane with its phases. They mocked the presumption of even-tempered beings and made promises that they would never fear the witch inside themselves. The women danced wildly as sparks broke away from the flames and entered the night sky as stars.

And they sang a song given to them by Shoshone grandmothers: 40

Ah ne nah, nah	Consider the rabbits
nin nah nah—	How gently they walk on the earth—
ah ne nah, nah	Consider the rabbits
nin nah nah—	How gently they walk on the earth—
Nyaga mutzi	We remember them
oh ne nay—	We can walk gently also—
Nyaga mutzi	We remember them
oh ne nay—	We can walk gently also—

The women danced and drummed and sang for weeks, preparing themselves for what was to come. They would reclaim the desert for the sake of their children, for the sake of the land.

A few miles downwind from the fire circle, bombs were being   41
tested. Rabbits felt the tremors. Their soft leather pads on paws, and feet recognized the shaking sands, while the roots of mesquite and sage were smoldering. Rocks were hot from the inside out and dust devils hummed unnaturally. And each time there was another nuclear test, ravens watched the desert heave. Stretch marks appeared. The land was losing its muscle.

The women couldn't bear it any longer. They were mothers. They   42
had suffered labor pains but always under the promise of birth. The red hot pains beneath the desert promised death only, as each bomb became a stillborn. A contract had been made and broken between human beings and the land. A new contract was being drawn by the women, who understood the fate of the earth as their own.

Under the cover of darkness, ten women slipped under a barbed-   43
wire fence and entered the contaminated country. They were trespassing. They walked toward the town of Mercury, in moonlight, taking their cues from coyote, kit fox, antelope squirrel, and quail. They moved quietly and deliberately through the maze of Joshua

trees. When a hint of daylight appeared they rested, drinking tea and sharing their rations of food. The women closed their eyes. The time had come to protest with the heart, that to deny one's genealogy with the earth was to commit treason against one's soul.

At dawn, the women draped themselves in mylar, wrapping long   44
streamers of silver plastic around their arms to blow in the breeze. They wore clear masks, that became the faces of humanity. And when they arrived at the edge of Mercury, they carried all the butterflies of a summer day in their wombs. They paused to allow their courage to settle.

The town that forbids pregnant women and children to enter be-   45
cause of radiation risks was asleep. The women moved through the streets as winged messengers, twirling around each other in slow motion, peeking inside homes and watching the easy sleep of men and women. They were astonished by such stillness and periodically would utter a shrill note or low cry just to verify life.

The residents finally awoke to these strange apparitions. Some   46
simply stared. Others called authorities, and in time, the women were apprehended by wary soldiers dressed in desert fatigues. They were taken to a white, square building on the other edge of Mercury. When asked who they were and why they were there, the women replied, "We are mothers and we have come to reclaim the desert for our children."

The soldiers arrested them. As the ten women were blindfolded   47
and handcuffed, they began singing:

You can't forbid us everything
You can't forbid us to think—
You can't forbid our tears to flow
And you can't stop the songs that we sing.

The women continued to sing louder and louder, until they heard the voices of their sisters moving across the mesa:

Ah ne nah, nah
nin nah nah—
Ah ne nah, nah
nin nah nah—
Nyaga mutzi
oh ne nay—
Nyaga mutzi
oh ne nay—

"Call for reinforcements," one soldier said.

"We have," interrupted one women, "we have—and you have no   48
idea of our numbers."

I crossed the line at the Nevada Test Site and was arrested with nine   49
other Utahns for trespassing on military lands. They are still conducting

nuclear tests in the desert. Ours was an act of civil disobedience. But as I walked toward the town of Mercury, it was more than a gesture of peace. It was a gesture on behalf of the Clan of One-Breasted Women.

As one officer cinched the handcuffs around my wrists, another 50
frisked my body. She found a pen and a pad of paper tucked inside my left boot.

"And these?" she asked sternly.   51

"Weapons," I replied.   52

Our eyes met. I smiled. She pulled the leg of my trousers back over 53
my boot.

"Step forward, please," she said as she took my arm.   54

We were booked under an afternoon sun and bused to Tonopah, 55
Nevada. It was a two-hour ride. This was familiar country. The Joshua trees standing their ground had been named by my ancestors, who believed they looked like prophets pointing west to the Promised Land. These were the same trees that bloomed each spring, flowers appearing like white flames in the Mojave. And I recalled a full moon in May, when Mother and I had walked among them, flushing out mourning doves and owls.

The bus stopped short of town. We were released.   56

The officials thought it was a cruel joke to leave us stranded in the 57
desert with no way to get home. What they didn't realize was that we were home, soul-centered and strong, women who recognized the sweet smell of sage as fuel for our spirits.

QUESTIONS FOR DISCUSSION

1　Why did the author's grandmother believe that a mastectomy can be "one of the most spiritual experiences you will ever encounter"? Why do you think that the author's mother looks radiant after her mastectomy and tells her children, "I felt the arms of God around me?"

2　What real-world physical event does the recurring dream of a "flash of light" in the desert night recall? What are the long-term, hidden consequences of this event?

3　What is Williams's purpose in writing this essay? Do you think that she would feel as her mother did if she were to develop breast cancer?

4　Why does Williams participate in the ritual protest in Mercury? What weapons does Williams have with her during the protest?

5　How does the officials' "cruel joke" on the protesters turn out differently than expected? In what sense are the women victorious, despite the physical defeat of their protest? With whose position are you in agreement? Explain your point of view.

IDEAS FOR WRITING

1   Write an essay about a political or social event that has had serious implications for the health of our natural world and of ourselves, as Williams has in this selection, or write about an event
you have participated in, witnessed, or studied that involved a
protest against some form of social injustice.

2   Write an essay that supports or refutes Williams's claim that "to
deny one's genealogy with the earth was to commit treason
against one's soul."

Environmental Issues:
Protection and Preservation

Thinking Like a Mountain

A LDO L EOPOLD

The thinking of Aldo Leopold (1886–1948), who was born and raised in Iowa, continues to influence the environmental movement. In 1909, Leopold was one of the first graduates from Yale University's Forestry School. He began his career as a ranger in the U.S. Forest Service and worked in forestry conservation in the Southwest until 1932, when he accepted the position of professor of wildlife management at the University of Wisconsin. President Franklin D. Roosevelt appointed Leopold to the Special Committee on Wildlife Restoration in 1934. Leopold also served as an adviser on conservation to the United Nations in 1948. Leopold's most widely read book, A Sand County Almanac *(1949), chronicles the seasons, following the migrations of wildlife to establish his principle that "a thing is right when it tends to preserve the integrity, stability, and beauty of the biotic community. It is wrong when it tends otherwise."* A Sand County Almanac, *from which the following selection is excerpted, continues to capture the interest of modern readers. Since republication in 1981, it has sold over 1 million copies.*

A deep chesty bawl echoes from rimrock to rimrock, rolls down the   1
mountain, and fades into the far blackness of the night. It is an out-
burst of wild defiant sorrow, and of contempt for all the adversities of
the world.

Every living thing (and perhaps many a dead one as well) pays heed   2
to that call. To the deer it is a reminder of the way of all flesh, to the
pine a forecast of midnight scuffles and of blood upon the snow, to
the coyote a promise of gleanings to come, to the cowman a threat of
red ink at the bank, to the hunter a challenge of fang against bullet. Yet
behind these obvious and immediate hopes and fears there lies a
deeper meaning, known only to the mountain itself. Only the mountain has lived long enough to listen objectively to the howl of a wolf.

Those unable to decipher the hidden meaning know nevertheless   3
that it is there, for it is felt in all wolf country, and distinguishes that
country from all other land. It tingles in the spine of all who hear
wolves by night, or who scan their tracks by day. Even without sight or
sound of wolf, it is implicit in a hundred small events: the midnight
whinny of a pack horse, the rattle of rolling rocks, the bound of a flee-
ing deer, the way shadows lie under the spruces. Only the ineducable
tyro can fail to sense the presence or absence of wolves, or the fact
that mountains have a secret opinion about them.

My own conviction on this score dates from the day I saw a wolf die.   4
We were eating lunch on a high rimrock, at the foot of which a turbu-
lent river elbowed its way. We saw what we thought was a doe fording

the torrent, her breast awash in white water. When she climbed the bank toward us and shook out her tail, we realized our error: it was a wolf. A half-dozen others, evidently grown pups, sprang from the willows and all joined in a welcoming mêlée of wagging tails and playful maulings. What was literally a pile of wolves writhed and tumbled in the center of an open flat at the foot of our rimrock.

In those days we had never heard of passing up a chance to kill a wolf. In a second we were pumping lead into the pack, but with more excitement than accuracy: how to aim a steep downhill shot is always confusing. When our rifles were empty, the old wolf was down, and a pup was dragging a leg into impassable slide-rocks. 5

We reached the old wolf in time to watch a fierce green fire dying in her eyes. I realized then, and have known ever since, that there was something new to me in those eyes—something known only to her and to the mountain. I was young then, and full of trigger-itch; I thought that because fewer wolves meant more deer, that no wolves would mean hunters' paradise. But after seeing the green fire die, I sensed that neither the wolf nor the mountain agreed with such a view. 6

Since then I have lived to see state after state extirpate its wolves. I have watched the face of many a newly wolfless mountain, and seen the south-facing slopes wrinkle with a maze of new deer trails. I have seen every edible bush and seedling browsed, first to anaemic desuetude, and then to death. I have seen every edible tree defoliated to the height of a saddlehorn. Such a mountain looks as if someone had given God a new pruning shears, and forbidden Him all other exercise. In the end the starved bones of the hoped-for deer herd, dead of its own too-much, bleach with the bones of the dead sage, or molder under the high-lined junipers. 7

I now suspect that just as a deer herd lives in mortal fear of its wolves, so does a mountain live in mortal fear of its deer. And perhaps with better cause, for while a buck pulled down by wolves can be replaced in two or three years, a range pulled down by too many deer may fail of replacement in as many decades. 8

So also with cows. The cowman who cleans his range of wolves does not realize that he is taking over the wolf's job of trimming the herd to fit the range. He has not learned to think like a mountain. Hence we have dustbowls, and rivers washing the future into the sea. 9

We all strive for safety, prosperity, comfort, long life, and dullness. The deer strives with his supple legs, the cowman with trap and poison, the statesman with pen, the most of us with machines, votes, and dollars, but it all comes to the same thing: peace in our time. A measure of success in this is all well enough, and perhaps is a requisite to objective thinking, but too much safety seems to yield only danger in the long run. Perhaps this is behind Thoreau's dictum: In wildness 10 is the [preservation] of the world. Perhaps this is the hidden meaning in the howl of the wolf, long known among mountains, but seldom perceived among men.

QUESTIONS FOR DISCUSSION

1   What did Leopold's title suggest to you before you read the selection?
2   Why might Leopold feel the need to personify the mountain? In what sense do mountains "think"?
3   Why do Leopold's thoughts and feelings about wolves change after hunting them? What do the green dying eyes of the wolf signify?
4   What do the mountains know about the wolves, cows, deer, and statesmen? Explain Leopold's claim: "Only the mountain has lived long enough to listen objectively to the howl of a wolf."
5   Why does Leopold believe that "in wildness is the [preservation] of the world"? Explain why you agree or disagree with his point of view.

IDEAS FOR WRITING

1   Write an essay that presents an extended definition of the word *wild*. Refer to Leopold, Henry David Thoreau, and Gary Snyder (whose essay is included in the last section of this book) to support your own point of view.
2   Write an essay that supports or refutes an environmental group's position on the preservation of an endangered species or land area.

The Obligation to Endure

RACHEL CARSON

*The writings of Rachel Carson (1907–1964) have been transform-
ing the way Americans think about environmental issues for over
thirty years. Born in Springfield, Pennsylvania, Carson completed
her undergraduate degree at Pennsylvanian College for Women and
her graduate studies at Johns Hopkins University. From 1936 to 1952,
she worked as a marine biologist with the U.S. Fish and Wildlife
Service in Washington, D.C. Then she turned her energies full-time
to her research and writing. Her first book,* Under the Sea-Wind:
A Naturalist's Picture of Ocean Life *(1941), was widely read because
it made the facts of science understandable and exciting. The* Sea
Around Us *(1951) became a national and international best-seller
and was translated into many languages. The* Edge of the Sea *(1954)
continued her exploration of marine life. Her best-known book,*
Silent Spring *(1962), from which the following selection is excerpted,
warns of the danger of the widespread use of DDT and other pesticides. This work continues to play an important role in current political and social opinions and legislation related to our environment.*

The history of life on earth has been a history of interaction be-   1
tween living things and their surroundings. To a large extent, the physical form and the habits of the earth's vegetation and its animal life
have been molded by the environment. Considering the whole span of
earthly time, the opposite effect, in which life actually modifies its surroundings, has been relatively slight. Only within the moment of time
represented by the present century has one species—man—acquired
significant power to alter the nature of his world.

During the past quarter century this power has not only increased   2
to one of disturbing magnitude but it has changed in character. The
most alarming of all man's assaults upon the environment is the contamination of air, earth, rivers, and sea with dangerous and even
lethal materials. This pollution is for the most part irrecoverable; the
chain of evil it initiates not only in the world that must support life but
in living tissues is for the most part irreversible. In this now universal
contamination of the environment, chemicals are the sinister and
little-recognized partners of radiation in changing the very nature of
the world—the very nature of its life. Strontium 90, released through
nuclear explosions into the air, comes to earth in rain or drifts down
as fallout, lodges in soil, enters into the grass or corn or wheat grown
there, and in time takes up its abode in the bones of a human being,
there to remain until his death. Similarly, chemicals sprayed on crop-
lands or forests or gardens lie long in soil, entering into living organisms, passing from one to another in a chain of poisoning and death.

Or they pass mysteriously by underground streams until they emerge and, through the alchemy of air and sunlight, combine into new forms that kill vegetation, sicken cattle, and work unknown harm on those who drink from once pure wells. As Albert Schweitzer has said, "Man can hardly even recognize the devils of his own creation."

It took hundreds of millions of years to produce the life that now   3
inhabits the earth—eons of time in which that developing and evolving and diversifying life reached a state of adjustment and balance with its surroundings. The environment, rigorously shaping and directing the life it supported, contained elements that were hostile as well as supporting. Certain rocks gave out dangerous radiation; even within the light of the sun, from which all life draws its energy, there were short-wave radiations with power to injure. Given time— time not in years but in millennia—life adjusts, and a balance has been reached. For time is the essential ingredient; but in the modern world there is no time.

The rapidity of change and the speed with which new situations are   4
created follow the impetuous and heedless pace of man rather than the deliberate pace of nature. Radiation is no longer merely the background radiation of rocks, the bombardment of cosmic rays, the ultraviolet of the sun that have existed before there was any life on earth; radiation is now the unnatural creation of man's tampering with the atom. The chemicals to which life is asked to make its adjustment are no longer merely the calcium and silica and copper and all the rest of the minerals washed out of the rocks and carried in rivers to the sea; they are the synthetic creations of man's inventive mind, brewed in his laboratories, and having no counterparts in nature.

To adjust to these chemicals would require time on the scale that is   5
nature's; it would require not merely the years of a man's life but the life of generations. And even this, were it by some miracle possible, would be futile, for the new chemicals come from our laboratories in an endless stream; almost five hundred annually find their way into actual use in the United States alone. The figure is staggering and its implications are not easily grasped—500 new chemicals to which the bodies of men and animals are required somehow to adapt each year, chemicals totally outside the limits of biologic experience.

Among them are many that are used in man's war against nature.   6
Since the mid-1940's over 200 basic chemicals have been created for use in killing insects, weeds, rodents, and other organisms described in the modern vernacular as "pests"; and they are sold under several thousand different brand names.

These sprays, dusts, and aerosols are now applied almost univer-   7
sally to farms, gardens, forests, and homes—nonselective chemicals that have the power to kill every insect, the "good" and the "bad," to still the song of birds and the leaping of fish in the streams, to coat the leaves with a deadly film, and to linger on in soil—all this though the

intended target may be only a few weeds or insects. Can anyone believe it is possible to lay down such a barrage of poisons on the surface of the earth without making it unfit for all life? They should not be called "insecticides," but "biocides."

The whole process of spraying seems caught up in an endless spiral. 8
Since DDT was released for civilian use, a process of escalation has been going on in which ever more toxic materials must be found. This has happened because insects, in a triumphant vindication of Darwin's principle of the survival of the fittest, have evolved super races immune to the particular insecticide used, hence a deadlier one has always to be developed—and then a deadlier one than that. It has happened also because . . . destructive insects often undergo a "flareback," or resurgence, after spraying, in numbers greater than before. Thus the chemical war is never won, and all life is caught in its violent crossfire.

Along with the possibility of the extinction of mankind by nuclear 9
war, the central problem of our age has therefore become the contamination of man's total environment with such substances of incredible potential for harm—substances that accumulate in the tissues of plants and animals and even penetrate the germ cells to shatter or alter the very material of heredity upon which the shape of the future depends.

Some would-be architects of our future look toward a time when it 10
will be possible to alter the human germ plasm by design. But we may easily be doing so now by inadvertence, for many chemicals, like radiation, bring about gene mutations. It is ironic to think that man might determine his own future by something so seemingly trivial as the choice of an insect spray.

All this has been risked—for what? Future historians may well be 11
amazed by our distorted sense of proportion. How could intelligent beings seek to control a few unwanted species by a method that contaminated the entire environment and brought the threat of disease and death even to their own kind? Yet this is precisely what we have done. We have done it, moreover, for reasons that collapse the moment we examine them. We are told that the enormous and expanding use of pesticides is necessary to maintain farm production. Yet is our real problem not one of *overproduction?* Our farms, despite measures to remove acreages from production and to pay farmers *not* to produce, have yielded such a staggering excess of crops that the American taxpayer in 1962 is paying out more than one billion dollars a year as the total carrying cost of the surplus-food storage program. And is the situation helped when one branch of the Agriculture Department tries to reduce production while another states, as it did in 1958, "It is believed generally that reduction of crop acreages under provisions of the Soil Bank will stimulate interest in use of chemicals to obtain maximum production on the land retained in crops."

All this is not to say there is no insect problem and no need of con-   12
trol. I am saying, rather, that control must be geared to realities, not to
mythical situations, and that the methods employed must be such
that they do not destroy us along with the insects.

The problem whose attempted solution has brought such a train of   13
disaster in its wake is an accompaniment of our modern way of life.
Long before the age of man, insects inhabited the earth—a group of
extraordinarily varied and adaptable beings. Over the course of time
since man's advent, a small percentage of the more than half a million
species of insects have come into conflict with human welfare in two
principal ways: as competitors for the food supply and as carriers of
human disease.

Disease-carrying insects become important where human beings   14
are crowded together, especially under conditions where sanitation is
poor, as in time of natural disaster or war or in situations of extreme
poverty and deprivation. Then control of some sort becomes necessary. It is a sobering fact, however, . . . that the method of massive
chemical control has had only limited success, and also threatens to
worsen the very conditions it is intended to curb.

Under primitive agricultural conditions the farmer had few insect   15
problems. These arose with the intensification of agriculture—the
devotion of immense acreages to a single crop. Such a system set the
stage for explosive increases in specific insect populations. Single-
crop farming does not take advantage of the principles by which
nature works; it is agriculture as an engineer might conceive it to be.
Nature has introduced great variety into the landscape, but man has
displayed a passion for simplifying it. Thus he undoes the built-in
checks and balances by which nature holds the species within
bounds. One important natural check is a limit on the amount of suit-
able habitat for each species. Obviously then, an insect that lives on
wheat can build up its population to much higher levels on a farm devoted to wheat than on one in which wheat is intermingled with other
crops to which the insect is not adapted.

The same thing happens in other situations. A generation or more   16
ago, the towns of large areas of the United States lined their streets
with the noble elm tree. Now the beauty they hopefully created is
threatened with complete destruction as disease sweeps through the
elms, carried by a beetle that would have only limited chance to build
up large populations and to spread from tree to tree if the elms were
only occasional trees in a richly diversified planting.

Another factor in the modern insect problem is one that must be   17
viewed against a background of geologic and human history: the
spreading of thousands of different kinds of organisms from their
native homes to invade new territories. This worldwide migration
has been studied and graphically described by the British ecologist

Charles Elton in his recent book *The Ecology of Invasions*. During the Cretaceous Period, some hundred million years ago, flooding seas cut many land bridges between continents and living things found themselves confined in what Elton calls "colossal separate nature reserves." There, isolated from others of their kind, they developed many new species. When some of the land masses were joined again, about 15 million years ago, these species began to move out into new territories—a movement that is not only still in progress but is now receiving considerable assistance from man.

The importation of plants is the primary agent in the modern spread of species, for animals have almost invariably gone along with the plants, quarantine being a comparatively recent and not completely effective innovation. The United States Office of Plant Introduction alone has introduced almost 200,000 species and varieties of plants from all over the world. Nearly half of the 180 or so major insect enemies of plants in the United States are accidental imports from abroad, and most of them have come as hitchhikers on plants.   18

In new territory, out of reach of the restraining hand of the natural enemies that kept down its numbers in its native land, an invading plant or animal is able to become enormously abundant. Thus it is no accident that our most troublesome insects are introduced species.   19

These invasions, both the naturally occurring and those dependent on human assistance, are likely to continue indefinitely. Quarantine and massive chemical campaigns are only extremely expensive ways of buying time. We are faced, according to Dr. Elton, "with a life-and-death need not just to find new technological means of suppressing this plant or that animal"; instead we need the basic knowledge of animal populations and their relations to their surroundings that will "promote an even balance and damp down the explosive power of outbreaks and new invasions."   20

Much of the necessary knowledge is now available but we do not use it. We train ecologists in our universities and even employ them in our governmental agencies but we seldom take their advice. We allow the chemical death rain to fall as though there were no alternative, whereas in fact there are many, and our ingenuity could soon discover many more if given opportunity.   21

Have we fallen into a mesmerized state that makes us accept as inevitable that which is inferior or detrimental, as though having lost the will or the vision to demand that which is good? Such thinking, in the words of the ecologist Paul Shepard, "idealizes life with only its head out of water, inches above the limits of toleration of the corruption of its own environment . . . Why should we tolerate a diet of weak poisons, a home in insipid surroundings, a circle of acquaintances who are not quite our enemies, the noise of motors with just enough relief to prevent insanity? Who would want to live in a world which is just not quite fatal?"   22

Yet such a world is pressed upon us. The crusade to create a chem- 23
ically sterile, insect-free world seems to have engendered a fanatic
zeal on the part of many specialists and most of the so-called control
agencies. On every hand there is evidence that those engaged in
spraying operations exercise a ruthless power. "The regulatory ento-
mologists . . . function as prosecutor, judge and jury, tax assessor and
collector and sheriff to enforce their own orders," said Connecticut
entomologist Neely Turner. The most flagrant abuses go unchecked in
both state and federal agencies.

It is not my contention that chemical insecticides must never be 24
used. I do contend that we have put poisonous and biologically
potent chemicals indiscriminately into the hands of persons largely
or wholly ignorant of their potentials for harm. We have subjected
enormous numbers of people to contact with these poisons, without
their consent and often without their knowledge. If the Bill of Rights
contains no guarantee that a citizen shall be secure against lethal
poisons distributed either by private individuals or by public officials,
it is surely only because our forefathers, despite their considerable
wisdom and foresight, could conceive of no such problem.

I contend, furthermore, that we have allowed these chemicals to be 25
used with little or no advance investigation of their effect on soil,
water, wildlife, and man himself. Future generations are unlikely to
condone our lack of prudent concern for the integrity of the natural
world that supports all life.

There is still very limited awareness of the nature of the threat. This 26
is an era of specialists, each of whom sees his own problem and is
unaware of or intolerant of the larger frame into which it fits. It is also
an era dominated by industry, in which the right to make a dollar at
whatever cost is seldom challenged. When the public protests, con-
fronted with some obvious evidence of damaging results of pesticide
applications, it is fed little tranquilizing pills of half truth. We urgently
need an end to these false assurances, to the sugar coating of un-
palatable facts. It is the public that is being asked to assume the risks
that the insect controllers calculate. The public must decide whether
it wishes to continue on the present road, and it can do so only when
in full possession of the facts. In the words of Jean Rostand, "The
obligation to endure gives us the right to know."

QUESTIONS FOR DISCUSSION

1   Why is Carson concerned about the contamination of the environment? How does she use Albert Schweitzer's idea to reinforce
her point of view?

2   Where is Carson's thesis most clearly stated? Do you agree or disagree with it? Explain your point of view.

3   Why does Carson put human power to control the environment into a historical perspective? Why does she believe that the use of insecticides is shortsighted? Explain why you agree or disagree with Carson.

4   Why do you think Carson has entitled this selection "The Obligation to Endure"?

5   In what ways has Carson's essay, written in 1962, been prophetic? Which of the problems that she anticipated have been solved? Which still need to be solved?

IDEAS FOR WRITING

1   Write an argument in response to Carson's assertion that the contamination of the environment may "shatter or alter the very material of heredity upon which the shape of the future depends."

2   Write a letter to the editor of your local paper that defines an environmental problem in your community and offers strategies for solving the problem.

Decimation by Poachers

DIAN FOSSEY

*Dian Fossey is remembered as the leader of the struggle to
preserve the mountain gorillas of Rwanda. Born in San Francisco,
Fossey (1932–1985) earned her B.A. from San Jose State University in
1954 and completed her Ph.D. in 1976 at Cambridge University. In
1955, Fossey moved to Kentucky, where she worked as an occupational
therapist for over ten years. Her fascination with mountain gorillas
led her to visit Louis Leakey at an archaeological excavation in
Tanzania. Fossey moved to Rwanda, worked with Leakey, and soon
began to develop studies of her own. In 1967 she established the
Karisoke Research Center to study the mountain gorilla population in
the Virunga Mountains of Rwanda. The center grew over a seventeen-
year period, with Fossey serving as its scientific director. She wrote*
Gorillas in the Mist *(1983) to help preserve the mountain gorilla population. She was murdered in 1985 while trying to protect the gorillas
from poachers. In 1988, the book was adapted into a popular movie.
The selection that follows captures Fossey's immediate reaction and
longer-range responses after learning that poachers had killed one
of the gorillas that she had studied and loved.*

The holiday season with its annual threat of increased encroach-   1
ment within the park was approaching. My usual dread of this time of
the year was somewhat alleviated because our patrols had been quite
successful in confiscating poachers' weapons and in demolishing
traps. However, limited staff and funds meant we could cover only so
much of the extensive saddle area at any one time. We therefore alter-
nated the regions patrolled on a regular basis.

January 1, 1978, Nemeye returned to camp very late in the day to   2
announce that he had not been able to find Group 4. Their trail had
merged into numerous buffalo, elephant, poacher, and dog trails.
Fearful, he added that he had also found a great deal of blood along
the trails, as well as diarrhetic gorilla dung. In spite of the evidence of
poachers and dogs, Nemeye had shown a commendable amount of
courage in tracking Group 4 along their two-mile flee route back to
Visoke's slopes. The following day, four of us—Ian Redmond, accompanied by Nemeye, and myself, accompanied by Kanyaragana, the
houseman—left camp at dawn to begin searching for whatever the
vast saddle area might reveal.

It was Ian who found Digit's mutilated corpse lying in the corner of   3
a blood-soaked area of flattened vegetation. Digit's head and hands
had been hacked off; his body bore multiple spear wounds. Ian and
Nemeye left the corpse to search for me and Kanyaragana, patrolling

in another section. They wanted to tell us of the catastrophe so that I would not discover Digit's body myself.

There are times when one cannot accept facts for fear of shattering one's being. As I listened to Ian's news all of Digit's life, since my first meeting with him as a playful little ball of black fluff ten years earlier, passed through my mind. From that moment on, I came to live within an insulated part of myself.

4

Digit, long vital to his group as a sentry, was killed in this service by poachers on December 31, 1977. That day Digit took five mortal spear wounds into his body, held off six poachers and their dogs in order to allow his family members, including his mate Simba and their unborn infant, to flee to the safety of Visoke's slopes. Digit's last battle had been a lonely and courageous one. During his valiant struggle he managed to kill one of the poachers' dogs before dying. I have tried not to allow myself to think of Digit's anguish, pain, and the total comprehension he must have suffered in knowing what humans were doing to him.

5

Porters carried Digit's body back to camp, where it was buried several dozen yards in front of my cabin. To bury his body was not to bury his memory. That evening Ian Redmond and I debated two alternatives: bury Digit and retain the news of his slaughter or publicize his death to gain additional support for active conservation in the Parc des Volcans through regular and frequent patrols to rid the park of encroachers.

6

Ian, relatively new to the field, held optimistic views about all that could be gained by publicizing Digit's death. He felt that a public outcry over the needless slaughter would exert pressure on Rwandese government officials to imprison poachers for prolonged periods. He also believed that the incident might compel a greater degree of cooperation between Rwanda and Zaire so that the contiguous sections of the Virungas could function as one.

7

I did not share Ian's optimism. By the time of Digit's death I had been working eleven years in the Virungas. I had met only a handful of park guards or park officials who had not fallen victim to the general inertia and malaise of their poor and overpopulated countries. Indeed, one of the greatest drawbacks of the Virungas is that it is shared by three countries, each of which has problems far more urgent than the protection of wild animals. I did concur with Ian that an indignant public outcry might well result in large sums of unchanneled conservation money pouring into Rwanda, but little would be intended for active antipoacher patrols. Following the captures of Coco and Pucker, both funding and a new Land-Rover had been obtained by the Rwandese officials connected with the park at that time; however, neither financing nor Land-Rover was applied toward the park interests. I had come to believe that self-motivation must necessarily accompany monetary assistance if long-term goals were to be accomplished. My

8

greatest fear was that the world would climb evangelistically onto a "save the gorilla" bandwagon upon hearing of Digit's death. Was Digit to be the first sacrificial victim from the study groups if monetary rewards were to follow the news of his slaughter? This was my line of reasoning as Ian and I continued to discuss the pros and cons of publicizing Digit's death.

The black night skies faded into those of a gray-misted dawn when I realized that, like Ian, I did not want Digit to have died in vain. I decided to launch a Digit Fund to support active conservation of gorillas, the money only to be used to expand antipoacher foot patrols within the park. This would involve the recruitment, training, outfitting, and remuneration of Africans willing to work long tedious hours cutting down traplines and confiscating poacher weapons such as spears, bows, and arrows. I would have preferred to employ park guards for such work. Cooperation with the government is essential, especially when one is a guest in a foreign country. The park guards, not I, have the legal right to capture poachers, and they could also have used the extra income to supplement their monthly salaries of about sixty dollars. However, the park guards ostensibly work for the Parc des Volcans' Conservator, who is in turn employed by the Director of the Rwandese national parks and located in Kigali. The guards routinely receive their salaries whether they go into the park or not; thus this aspect of motivation had never worked successfully. For many years, I had returned to Rwanda after brief trips to America laden with boxes of new boots, uniforms, knapsacks, and tents for the guards. I had tried countless times to encourage the men to participate actively in antipoacher patrols conducted from Karisoke in the heartland of the park. The uniforms and boots, of course, were eagerly received, likewise the extra money paid and the food eaten at camp, but the guards' brief efforts were meaningless. The men wanted only to return as rapidly as possible to their villages and the local *pombe* bars, where most of the boots were sold to more affluent Rwandese in order to buy more *pombe.* My naive attitude eventually ceased once I came to realize that the long-standing poachers of the park are on extremely good terms with the guards, whom they regularly pay either in francs or meat for permission to hunt in the park. I also learned that the men the guards pretended to have captured during their stays at Karisoke were, in actual fact, friends or relatives who always managed to "escape" when being escorted to prison. I had made the mistake of paying the guards extra for each poacher caught instead of paying a flat salary for each day's work. This was a mistake I never repeated when later working with non-park-related recruitments, the only men I could personally motivate to work honestly and effectively. It was equally futile to pay a bonus for each trap snare brought to camp, since this practice only encouraged the manufacture of nooses to be brought to camp in exchange for the reward.

9

For several days Ian, the camp staff, and I backtracked the poachers' 10
trail to and from Digit's death site and maintained brief contacts with
Group 4—well secluded on Visoke's slopes—while mulling over the
decision we had to make. We found that Digit had not been killed for
the trophies of his head and hands as we originally had thought. Six
poachers had been working their trapline before inadvertently running into Group 4 at the line's end. Digit's body lay only 80 feet from the
last trap and some 260 feet from Group 4's day-nesting site where he
had been alone on sentry duty.

Tracking along the poachers' trail showed that the men had been 11
in the park killing antelope and setting traps for two days before en-
countering Group 4. They then fled back to the notorious poacher
Munyarukiko's village of Kidengezi, adjacent to Karisimbi's eastern
slopes. The poachers took Digit's head and hands as afterthoughts,
because such items had previously been sold profitably to Europeans.
Our original mistaken belief that Digit had been killed only for trophies is regretted. It continues to capture the public's imagination far
more than the actual truth: Digit was not killed as an intended victim
of slaughter by trophy hunters; he gave his life to save his family—
which, tragically, had been in the wrong place at the wrong time,
especially on New Year's Eve. If Digit's death proved to be an economic
boon to the park system, I wondered just how long Group 4 could
survive—a month? six months? a year? I awakened each morning
wondering who would be next.

Ian and I finally decided to publicize Digit's slaughter. A few days 12
later North American television viewers heard Walter Cronkite announce Digit's death on the "CBS Evening News." The Rwandese park
Conservator was invited to camp to see Digit's body before it was
buried. He arrived with Paulin Nkubili. The Chef des Brigades was
genuinely horrified at the mutilated corpse and promised to do all
that he could to apprehend any known poachers his men might
encounter in Ruhengeri. Active law enforcement is what active conservation is all about.

Six days following Digit's slaying, I was typing in my cabin when I 13
heard the woodman scream *"Bawindagi! Bawindagi!"*—"Poacher!
Poacher!" The four Rwandese working at camp immediately took up
the chase of an unknown man who had crept into camp attempting to
kill one of the many antelope now thriving in the security Karisoke
offered. After a long chase, the poacher was caught and brought back
to my cabin. The man was wearing a yellow T-shirt extensively stained
and sprayed with dried blood. He was also carrying a blood-stained
bow and five arrows. Questioning revealed that this was indeed the
blood of Digit.

The Chef des Brigades again climbed to camp with armed com- 14
mandos to take legal custody of the poacher, who was later tried,
convicted, and sentenced to prison in Ruhengeri. While at Karisoke,

Nkubili questioned the man and obtained the names of the other five poachers responsible for killing Digit. Within a week two of them had been captured. Three leading poachers of the Virungas—Munyarukiko, Sebahutu, and Gashabizi—eluded capture by hiding in the forest.

I resumed my contacts with Group 4 but, for countless weeks un-   15 able to accept the finality of Digit's death, I found myself looking toward the periphery of the group for the courageous young silver-back. The gorillas allowed me to share their proximity as before. This was a privilege that I felt I no longer deserved.

Tiger and Beetsme attempted to take Digit's place as Group 4 sen-   16 ries. However, the two young males frequently were diverted by their roughhouse wrestling games, leaving Uncle Bert to bear full responsi-bility for group security. Shortly after their flight to Visoke's slopes, Group 4 were harried by interaction attempts from Nunkie. Uncle Bert led his family back to the saddle area to get away from the per-sistence of the older silverback, who appeared to be trying to obtain Simba. Group 4 went directly to Digit's death site, circling the area for days as if looking for Digit, whose slaying, of course, they had not witnessed. Their actions were surprising to me. Over the previous ten years of research, whenever gorillas had encountered cattle herds, traps, or poachers, they usually avoided immediately returning to the areas that had threatened danger.

QUESTIONS FOR DISCUSSION

1   How does Dian Fossey first respond when she learns that Digit has been killed?

2   Why does Fossey initially think that she should not publicize Digit's death? Why does she change her mind? What are her goals for the Digit Fund?

3   Why do you think Digit was killed? How did reading about his death affect you?

4   What are your thoughts and feelings about Dian Fossey's devo-tion to the gorilla families? Do you agree that being physically close to the gorillas is "a privilege"?

5   How effective do you think that Fossey's lifetime efforts have been?

IDEAS FOR WRITING

1   Do some research into Fossey's struggle to protect the gorilla population in East Africa. Write a paper that discusses the impact of her work.

2   Write a paper about a person who has had a deep devotion to a particular animal and has helped to protect that animal in a unique and effective way.

student essay

Dian Fossey and Me

LINDSEY MUNRO

Originally from Sacramento, California, Lindsey Munro wrote this essay after completing a longer research project on the life of Dian Fossey. An international relations major, Munro is especially interested in environmental and developmental policy. Through an outreach program, she shares her love of nature with the elementary school children she visits weekly. As a staff writer of the Stanford Daily *(a student newspaper), she has many opportunities to express her opinions. In the following essay, Munro reflects on how she has come to realize that she can admire Fossey's courage and accomplishments as a champion of the mountain gorillas while not accepting Fossey's radical perspective on the preservation of wildlife.*

So many of us young people seek a hero. Usually our heroes share our passions and epitomize the kind of people we want to be. As I am concerned about the welfare of wildlife, Dian Fossey is certainly a hero of mine. When Fossey began her field work only 242 gorillas survived in the Virunga mountains; they were dangerously approaching extinction. To save the "gentle giants" Fossey spent 17 years living in the somewhat makeshift Karisoke Research Center she established. Most of these were lonely years, as Fossey was separated from her family and friends back in the United States; she was isolated even from most of the local people who did not live in the high altitudes of the mountain gorillas' habitat. Not only did Fossey sacrifice comfort and companionship high up in the Virungas, she also sacrificed her own safety by fighting for the gorillas' sake against the poachers and corrupt Rwandan government officials. Looking at her life and tragic murder by a still unidentified enemy, I am inspired by the legacy of unlimited courage and devotion that she has left for the world.

Yet Fossey has left a legacy that I cannot wholly accept. Fossey belonged to the school of conservationists that are better called preservationists because of their romantic view of nature. Preservationists believe nature should not be in any way spoiled by the world of humans. Such was the attitude Fossey expressed with her insistence that those students and employees who worked with her gorillas "must remember that the rights of the animal supersede human interests" (Fossey 14). Fossey's inability to compromise her preservationist ideals conflicts with my conservationist view that we must consider different perspectives when trying to save threatened wildlife; most important, we must consider the perspectives of the people who live with the wildlife. Although her commitment truly is inspiring, I cannot agree with Fossey that the needs of all humans must be subordinate to those of wildlife. The issue of wildlife tourism illustrates why my opinion must differ from Fossey's.

Fossey cherished the wild, uncorrupted environment of the Virun-   3
gas. With every new tourist center built to bring wealthy Westerners to the habitat of the mountain gorillas, she felt the mountains were corrupted by the artificial "civilized" world (22). Conceding that tourism could provide much-needed revenue to Rwanda (241), Fossey still insisted that promotion of tourism was only "theoretical" conservation. "Active conservation" was the only approach that Fossey believed could really save the gorillas from the brink of extinction (242). Fossey believed that active conservation means doing whatever necessary to stop all immediate threats to the gorillas, including "frequent patrols in wildlife areas to destroy poacher equipment and weapons" (242). Such methods need to be "supplemented by longer term projects" such as tourism, indicating that any such efforts to promote a tourist industry were of secondary importance.

Dividing conservation methods between "active" and "theoretical"   4
implies that tourism is of minor importance in the fight to preserve the gorillas, as well as elephants and other wildlife all over Africa. Idealistically I agree that the wildlife ought to come first, and that efforts to save animals in their natural habitat should prevail over all other considerations. The preservationist within me finds the idea of using tours and safaris to profit off the animals distasteful; likewise, I hate to see the pristine mountain world of the gorillas or the savannas of the elephants invaded by gawking, noisy tourists eager to snap some pictures.

Yet I cannot help but be realistic. My concern for the marginalized   5
people living with wildlife in places like Rwanda prevents me from staunchly following Fossey's idealistic position. Living in a nice house in a safe, economically advantaged area, it is easy for me to agree that the needs of the animals must be held above all else. However, for a poor African living in an impoverished, unhealthy, and crowded area Fossey's romantic ideals hold little meaning. For example, a campaign by Kenyans protesting the preservationist approach of Kenya's wildlife policy has the slogan, "Stop policies that put more value on elephants than on human beings" (Herman and Moldway 41). Tribal leader William Ole Ntimama reflects the view of many Africans who argue that the needs of people living with wildlife are ignored, saying, "Our people have always lived alongside the wildlife. Now we hate it" (qtd. in Herman and Moldway 42).

This conflict between preservationist and conservationist ap-   6
proaches to wildlife is occurring throughout Africa today. Conservationists believe wildlife tourism is the best way to help wildlife to pay for themselves. Most Africans do not benefit from living wildlife, and this puts the animals in danger because the Africans will kill them to survive. Elephants trample their crops and gorillas deprive Rwandans of much-needed space for agriculture or cattle grazing, while poaching gives Africans the opportunity to profit from dead animals; consequently

gorillas are hunted for their head and hands and African elephants are poached for their ivory.

By making wildlife tourism a viable industry, many conservationists hope to make living animals valuable to Africans. If tourists bring revenue to the underdeveloped areas, the people will benefit economically from conserving the animals rather than killing them. Thus, the wildlife can be protected while simultaneously helping the African people. The idea of making wildlife pay for itself runs contrary to Fossey's preservationist perspective. I, too, find the idea of assigning animals economic value somehow insulting to wildlife, but how can I not support the economic argument with the knowledge that nine out of ten Africans live in absolute poverty and that black Africa has the highest infant mortality rate in the world? How can I consider myself an ethical person if I only try to save wildlife while ignoring the tragic situation of millions of African people? I know that I cannot. Gorilla tours provided the third largest source of desperately needed foreign currency to Rwanda before war broke out in 1994 (Wallace 35). Since I cannot in good conscience adopt Fossey's uncompromising opinions and try to deny the Rwandan people this money that they need, I support tourism as one of the few ways to save both the wildlife and the people who live with it.

After careful consideration I am left with the conclusion that the wildness of wildlife must be made available to the tourism industry so that people will have incentives to keep the animals alive. While this conclusion is disheartening from the perspective of an idealistic preservationist, from the viewpoint of a conservationist who values people as well as wildlife, tourism provides hope that human and animal life can both be saved, each learning from one another, each making some sacrifices to live in harmony.

Knowing there are ways to succeed at the balancing act between the needs of people and the needs of the wildlife encourages me as I struggle to find my own way while also finding inspiration in Fossey's legacy. Compromising ideals is one of the most difficult things a human being must do; I understand why Fossey would not make compromises. I can admire her for never conceding. Most important, her life inspires me to strive to have the same strength as she had to fight for what one believes is right.

Works Cited

Fossey, Dian. *Gorillas in the Mist*. Boston: Houghton Mifflin, 1983.

Herman, Kai, and Milhaly Moldway. "Are Elephants Protected to Death?" *World Press Review*, April 1995: 41–42. First published in *Stern*, 19 January 1995.

Wallace, Bruce. "High Above It All: How War Brought Peace to Rwanda's Gorillas." *Maclean's*, 6 February 1995: 35.

QUESTIONS FOR DISCUSSION

1 Is there a person whom you consider a hero, even though you have some fundamental disagreements with the way this person lives (or lived) his or her life? How have you come to terms with the discrepancies between your hero and some of his or her actions with which you disagree?

2 Does the distinction that Munro makes between a preservationist and a conservationist help you to understand Fossey's total commitment to the preservation of the mountain gorillas?

3 How is Munro's argument structured? Is the structure effective?

4 Do you agree with Munro's point of view that the tourist industry in emerging African nations is important to their growth and well-being? Explain your point of view.

5 Do you agree with Munro's assertion that people must sometimes compromise their ideals? Do you agree that you can compromise your ideals without compromising yourself? Explain your response.

IDEAS FOR WRITING

1 Write an essay about a leader who has inspired you, or develop discussion question 2 into an essay.

2 Write a research paper that explores the impact of the tourist industry on a Third World country.

Nature and the
Philosophical Imagination

Nature

RALPH WALDO EMERSON

Ralph Waldo Emerson (1803–1882) is best known for his theories about the relationship between nature and the human soul. His sense of the mystical unity of nature is most clearly expressed in his philosophical work Nature *(1835). Emerson has been an inspiration to the major nature writers, including Henry David Thoreau, John Muir, and Aldo Leopold. Emerson attended Harvard as an undergraduate and then Harvard Divinity School from 1825 to 1827. Although he did not graduate, Emerson was offered a position as a pastor in Boston in 1829. After many theoretical disputes with his superiors, Emerson relinquished his position in 1833. He went on to form the Transcendental Club, which spoke out on crucial issues of the times, including slavery and women's suffrage. He also founded* Dial, *the magazine that served as a literary forum for the transcendental movement. Emerson's home in Concord, Massachusetts, was the gathering place for leading writers and thinkers of his time. The selection that follows is from* Nature.

> Nature is but an image or imitation of wisdom, the last thing of the soul; nature being a thing which doth only do, but not know.—Plotinus
>
> (MOTTO OF 1836)

> A subtle chain of countless rings
>
> The next unto the farthest brings;
>
> The eye reads omens where it goes,
>
> And speaks all languages the rose;
>
> And, striving to be man, the worm
>
> Mounts through all the spires of form.
>
> (MOTTO OF 1849)

Our age is retrospective. It builds the sepulchres of the fathers. It writes biographies, histories, and criticism. The foregoing generations beheld God and nature face to face; we, through their eyes. Why should not we also enjoy an original relation to the universe? Why should not we have a poetry and philosophy of insight and not of tradition, and a religion by revelation to us, and not the history of theirs? Embosomed for a season in nature, whose floods of life stream around and through us, and invite us, by the powers they supply, to action proportioned to nature, why should we grope among the dry bones of the past, or put the living generation into masquerade out of its faded wardrobe? The sun shines today also. There is more wool and flax in the fields. There are new lands, new men, new thoughts. Let us demand our own works and laws and worship.

Undoubtedly we have no questions to ask which are unanswerable.   2
We must trust the perfection of the creation so far as to believe that whatever curiosity the order of things has awakened in our minds, the order of things can satisfy. Every man's condition is a solution in hiero-glyphic to those inquiries he would put. He acts it as life, before he apprehends it as truth. In like manner, nature is already, in its forms and tendencies, describing its own design. Let us interrogate the great apparition that shines so peacefully around us. Let us inquire, to what end is nature?

All science has one aim, namely, to find a theory of nature. We have   3
theories of races and of functions, but scarcely yet a remote approach to an idea of creation. We are now so far from the road to truth, that religious teachers dispute and hate each other, and speculative men are esteemed unsound and frivolous. But to a sound judgment, the most abstract truth is the most practical. Whenever a true theory ap-pears, it will be its own evidence. Its test is, that it will explain all phenomena. Now many are thought not only unexplained but inex-plicable; as language, sleep, madness, dreams, beasts, sex.

Philosophically considered, the universe is composed of Nature   4
and the Soul. Strictly speaking, therefore, all that is separate from us, all which Philosophy distinguishes as the NOT ME, that is, both nature and art, all other men and my own body, must be ranked under this name, NATURE. In enumerating the values of nature and casting up their sum, I shall use the word in both senses;—in its common and in its philosophical import. In inquiries so general as our present one, the inaccuracy is not material; no confusion of thought will occur. *Nature,* in the common sense, refers to essences unchanged by man; space, the air, the river, the leaf. *Art* is applied to the mixture of his will with the same things, as in a house, a canal, a statue, a picture. But his operations taken together are so insignificant, a little chipping, baking, patching, and washing, that in an impression so grand as that of the world on the human mind, they do not vary the result.

To go into solitude, a man needs to retire as much from his chamber   5
as from society. I am not solitary whilst I read and write, though no-body is with me. But if a man would be alone, let him look at the stars. The rays that come from those heavenly worlds will separate between him and what he touches. One might think the atmosphere was made transparent with this design, to give man, in the heavenly bodies, the perpetual presence of the sublime. Seen in the streets of cities, how great they are! If the stars should appear one night in a thousand years,

how would men believe and adore; and preserve for many generations the remembrance of the city of God which had been shown! But every night come out these envoys of beauty, and light the universe with the admonishing smile.

The stars awaken a certain reverence, because though always present, they are inaccessible; but all natural objects make a kindred impression, when the mind is open to their influence. Nature never wears a mean appearance. Neither does the wisest man extort her secret, and lose his curiosity by finding out all of her perfection. Nature never became a toy to a wise spirit. The flowers, the animals, the mountains, reflected the wisdom of his best hour, as much as they had delighted the simplicity of his childhood.   6

When we speak of nature in this manner, we have a distinct but most poetical sense in the mind. We mean the integrity of impression made by manifold natural objects. It is this which distinguishes the stick of timber of the wood-cutter from the tree of the poet. The charming landscape which I saw this morning is indubitably made up of some twenty or thirty farms. Miller owns this field, Locke that, and Manning the woodland beyond. But none of them owns the landscape. There is a property in the horizon which no man has but he whose eye can integrate all the parts, that is, the poet. This is the best part of these men's farms, yet to this their warranty-deeds give no title.   7

To speak truly, few adult persons can see nature. Most persons do not see the sun. At least they have a very superficial seeing. The sun illuminates only the eye of the man, but shines into the eye and the heart of the child. The lover of nature is he whose inward and outward senses are still truly adjusted to each other; who has retained the spirit of infancy even into the era of manhood. His intercourse with heaven and earth becomes part of his daily food. In the presence of nature a wild delight runs through the man, in spite of real sorrows. Nature says,—he is my creature, and maugre all his impertinent griefs, he shall be glad with me. Not the sun or the summer alone, but every hour and season yields its tribute of delight; for every hour and change corresponds to and authorizes a different state of mind, from breathless noon to grimmest midnight. Nature is a setting that fits equally well a comic or a mourning piece. In good health, the air is a cordial of incredible virtue. Crossing a bare common, in snow puddles, at twilight, under a clouded sky, without having in my thoughts any occurrence of special good fortune, I have enjoyed a perfect exhilaration. I am glad to the brink of fear. In the woods, too, a man casts off his years, as the snake his slough, and at what period soever of life is always a child. In the woods is perpetual youth. Within these plantations of God, a decorum and sanctity reign, a perennial festival is dressed, and the guest sees not how he should tire of them in a thousand years. In the woods, we return to reason and faith. There I feel that nothing can befall me in life,—no disgrace, no calamity (leaving me my eyes),   8 which nature cannot repair. Standing on the bare ground,—my head bathed by the blithe air and uplifted into infinite space,—all mean egotism vanishes. I become a transparent eyeball; I am nothing; I see all; the currents of the Universal Being circulate through me; I am part or parcel of God. The name of the nearest friend sounds then foreign and accidental: to be brothers, to be acquaintances, master or servant, is then a trifle and a disturbance. I am the lover of uncontained and immortal beauty. In the wilderness, I find something more dear and connate than in streets or villages. In the tranquil landscape, and especially in the distant line of the horizon, man beholds somewhat as beautiful as his own nature.

The greatest delight which the fields and woods minister is the sug-   9
gestion of an occult relation between man and the vegetable. I am not alone and unacknowledged. They nod to me, and I to them. The waving of the boughs in the storm is new to me and old. It takes me by surprise, and yet is not unknown. Its effect is like that of a higher thought or a better emotion coming over me, when I deemed I was thinking justly or doing right.

Yet it is certain that the power to produce this delight does not   10
reside in nature, but in man, or in a harmony of both. It is necessary to use these pleasures with great temperance. For nature is not always tricked in holiday attire, but the same scene which yesterday breathed perfume and glittered as for the frolic of the nymphs is overspread with melancholy today. Nature always wears the colors of the spirit. To a man laboring under calamity, the heat of his own fire hath sadness in it. Then there is a kind of contempt of the landscape felt by him who has just lost by death a dear friend. The sky is less grand as it shuts down over less worth in the population.

QUESTIONS FOR DISCUSSION

1   How does Emerson define nature? What evidence does he use to develop his definition?

2   According to Emerson, how does an individual find solitude? What does solitude offer each individual? Do you agree with Emerson? Is solitude important in your life? Explain your response.

3   What understanding of nature does Emerson believe that the poet has that is greater than what the farmer or landlord owns? Do you agree or disagree with Emerson? Explain your answer.

4   According to Emerson, what qualities of mind and spirit must a person have to see nature truly? Explain why you agree or disagree.

5   Why does Emerson believe that "in the woods we return to reason and faith"? How does nature help Emerson to "be part or parcel of God"? How does nature reflect and heal a human's spirit?

IDEAS FOR WRITING

1 Write an essay in support of Emerson's conception of nature, or present an argument that refutes Emerson's theory. What are the implications and applications of his theory? Can modern men and women take heed of his advice? How?

2 Write about an adventure or experience in nature that provided you with spiritual nourishment and healing.

Walking

Henry David Thoreau

One of the fathers of the nature writing tradition and the modern ecological movement, Henry David Thoreau (1817–1862) was devoted to his family and his hometown of Concord, Massachusetts, where he lived all of his life. Known for his work as a naturalist, editor, political protestor, philosopher, and writer, Thoreau maintained the uncompromising belief that humans can better themselves and their government by looking inward, following inner principles, and searching for the connections between the natural world and the human spirit. Thoreau published his first book as a naturalist writer, A Week on the Concord and Merrimack Rivers, *in 1849, and the American classic* Walden: or Life in the Woods *in 1854. His best-known essay, "Civil Disobedience," eloquently presents his belief that private conscience rather than majority rule should form the standards for moral action. The following selection is from* Walking *(1862), which continues to be one of the conservation movement's basic texts.*

1   The West of which I speak is but another name for the Wild; and what I have been preparing to say is, that in Wildness is the preservation of the World. Every tree sends its fibres forth in search of the Wild. The cities import it at any price. Men plough and sail for it. From the forest and wilderness come the tonics and barks which brace mankind. Our ancestors were savages. The story of Romulus and Remus being suckled by a wolf is not a meaningless fable. The founders of every state which has risen to eminence have drawn their nourishment and vigor from a similar wild source. It was because the children of the Empire were not suckled by the wolf that they were conquered and displaced by the children of the northern forests who were.

2   I believe in the forest, and in the meadow, and in the night in which the corn grows. We require an infusion of hemlock-spruce or arborvitae in our tea. There is a difference between eating and drinking for strength and from mere gluttony. The Hottentots eagerly devour the marrow of the koodoo and other antelopes raw, as a matter of course. Some of our Northern Indians eat raw the marrow of the Arctic reindeer, as well as the various other parts, including the summits of the antlers, as long as they are soft. And herein, perchance, they have stolen a march on the cooks of Paris. They get what usually goes to feed the fire. This is probably better than stall-fed beef and slaughter-house pork to make a man of. Give me a wildness whose glance no civilization can endure,—as if we lived on the marrow of koodoos devoured raw.

3   There are some intervals which border the strain of the wood-thrush, to which I would migrate,—wild lands where no settler has squatted; to which, methinks, I am already acclimated.

The African hunter Cummings tells us that the skin of the eland, as well as that of most other antelopes just killed, emits the most delicious perfume of trees and grass. I would have every man so much like a wild antelope, so much a part and parcel of Nature, that his very person should thus sweetly advertise our senses of his presence, and remind us of those parts of Nature which he most haunts. I feel no disposition to be satirical, when the trapper's coat emits the odor of musquash even; it is a sweeter scent to me that that which commonly exhales from the merchant's or the scholar's garments. When I go into their wardrobes and handle their vestments, I am reminded of no grassy plains and flowery meads which they have frequented, but of dusty merchants' exchanges and libraries rather.

A tanned skin is something more than respectable, and perhaps olive is a fitter color than white for a man,—a denizen of the woods. "The pale white man!" I do not wonder that the African pitied him. Darwin the naturalist says, "A white man bathing by the side of a Tahitian was like a plant bleached by the gardener's art, compared with a fine, dark green one, growing vigorously in the open fields."

Ben Jonson exclaims,—

"How near to good is what is fair!"

So I would say,—

How near to good is what is *wild!*

Life consists with wildness. The most alive is the wildest. Not yet subdued to man, its presence refreshes him. One who pressed forward incessantly and never rested from his labors, who grew fast and made infinite demands on life, would always find himself in a new country or wilderness, and surrounded by the raw material of life. He would be climbing over the prostrate stems of primitive forest-trees.

Hope and the future for me are not in lawns and cultivated fields, not in towns and cities, but in the impervious and quaking swamps. When, formerly, I have analyzed my partiality for some farm which I had contemplated purchasing, I have frequently found that I was attracted solely by a few square rods of impermeable and unfathomable bog,—a natural sink in one corner of it. That was the jewel which dazzled me. I derive more of my subsistence from the swamps which surround my native town than from the cultivated gardens in the village. There are no richer parterres to my eyes than the dense beds of dwarf andromeda (*Cassandra calyculata*) which cover these tender places on the earth's surface. Botany cannot go farther than tell me the names of the shrubs which grow there,—the high-blueberry, panicled andromeda, lamb-kill, azalea, and rhodora—all standing in the quaking sphagnum. I often think that I should like to have my house front on this mass of dull red bushes, omitting other flower plots and borders, transplanted spruce and trim box, even graveled walks,—to have this fertile spot under my windows, not a few imported barrow-fulls of soil only to cover the sand which was thrown out in digging the cellar. Why not put my house, my parlor, behind this plot, instead of behind that meagre assemblage of curiosities, that poor apology for a Nature and Art, which I call my front yard? It is an effort to clear up and make a decent appearance when the carpenter and mason have departed, though done as much for the passer-by as the dweller within. The most tasteful front-yard fence was never an agreeable object of study to me; the most elaborate ornaments, acorn-tops, or what not, soon wearied and disgusted me. Bring your sills up to the very edge of the swamp, then (though it may not be the best place for a dry cellar), so that there be no access on that side to citizens. Front yards are not made to walk in, but, at most, through, and you could go in the back way.

Yes, though you may think me perverse, if it were proposed to me   8 to dwell in the neighborhood of the most beautiful garden that ever human art contrived, or else of a Dismal Swamp, I should certainly decide for the swamp. How vain, then, have been all your labors, citizens, for me!

My spirits infallibly rise in proportion to the outward dreariness.   9 Give me the ocean, the desert, or the wilderness! In the desert, pure air and solitude compensate for want of moisture and fertility. The traveler Burton says of it: "Your *morale* improves; you become frank and cordial, hospitable and single-minded. . . . In the desert, spirituous liquors excite only disgust. There is a keen enjoyment in a mere animal existence." They who have been traveling long on the steppes of Tartary say: "On reentering cultivated lands, the agitation, perplexity, and turmoil of civilization oppressed and suffocated us; the air seemed to fail us, and we felt every moment as if about to die of asphyxia." When I would recreate myself, I seek the darkest wood, the thickest and most interminable and, to the citizen, most dismal swamp. I enter a swamp as a sacred place,—a *sanctum sanctorum*. There is the strength, the marrow of Nature. The wild-wood covers the virgin-mould,—and the same soil is good for men and for trees. A man's health requires as many acres of meadow to his prospect as his farm does loads of muck. There are the strong meats on which he feeds. A town is saved, not more by the righteous men in it than by the woods and swamps that surround it. A township where one primitive forest waves above while another primitive forest rots below,— such a town is fitted to raise not only corn and potatoes, but poets and philosophers for the coming ages. In such a soil grew Homer and Confucius and the rest, and out of such a wilderness comes the Reformer eating locusts and wild honey.

To preserve wild animals implies generally the creation of a forest   10 for them to dwell in or resort to. So it is with man. A hundred years ago they sold bark in our streets peeled from our own woods. In the very aspect of those primitive and rugged trees there was, methinks, a tanning principle which hardened and consolidated the fibres of men's thoughts. Ah! already I shudder for these comparatively degenerate days of my native village, when you cannot collect a load of bark of good thickness,—and we no longer produce tar and turpentine.

The civilized nations—Greece, Rome, England—have been sustained by the primitive forests which anciently rotted where they stand. They survive as long as the soil is not exhausted. Alas for human culture! little is to be expected of a nation, when the vegetable mould is exhausted, and it is compelled to make manure of the bones of its fathers. There the poet sustains himself merely by his own superfluous fat, and the philosopher comes down on his marrow-bones. 11

It is said to be the task of the American "to work the virgin soil," and that "agriculture here already assumes proportions unknown everywhere else." I think that the farmer displaces the Indian even because he redeems the meadow, and so makes himself stronger and in some respects more natural. I was surveying for a man the other day a single straight line one hundred and thirty-two rods long, through a swamp, at whose entrance might have been written the words which Dante read over the entrance to the infernal regions,—"Leave all hope, ye that enter,"—that is, of ever getting out again; where at one time I saw my employer actually up to his neck and swimming for his life in his property, though it was still winter. He had another similar swamp which I could not survey at all, because it was completely under water, and nevertheless, with regard to a third swamp, which I did *survey* from a distance, he remarked to me, true to his instincts, that he would not part with it for any consideration, on account of the mud which it contained. And that man intends to put a girdling ditch round the whole in the course of forty months, and so redeem it by the magic of his spade. I refer to him only as the type of a class. 12

The weapons with which we have gained our most important victories, which should be handed down as heirlooms from father to son, are not the sword and the lance, but the bushwhack, the turf-cutter, the spade, and the boghoe, rusted with the blood of many a meadow, and begrimed with the dust of many a hard-fought field. The very winds blew the Indian's corn-field into the meadow, and pointed out the way which he had not the skill to follow. He had no better implement with which to intrench himself in the land than a clam-shell. But the farmer is armed with plough and spade. 13

In literature it is only the wild that attracts us. Dullness is but another name for tameness. It is the uncivilized free and wild thinking in "Hamlet" and the "Iliad," in all the Scriptures and Mythologies, not learned in the schools, that delights us. As the wild duck is more swift and beautiful than the tame, so is the wild—the mallard—thought, which 'mid falling dews wings its way above the fens. A truly good book is something as natural, and as unexpectedly and unaccountably fair 14 and perfect, as a wild flower discovered on the prairies of the West or in the jungles of the East. Genius is a light which makes the darkness visible, like the lightning's flash, which perchance shatters the temple of knowledge itself,—and not a taper lighted at the hearthstone of the race, which pales before the light of common day.

QUESTIONS FOR DISCUSSION

1   How does Thoreau define the "wild"? Why does he believe that it is central to man's well-being?

2   Why does Thoreau find hope for the future in the swamps that surround his village rather than in its cultivated gardens? Why would he prefer to have his house front on a swamp?

3   Do you agree with Thoreau when he claims, "A man's health requires as many acres of meadow to his prospect as his farm does loads of muck"? In what sense does Thoreau use the word *health*?

4   Why is Thoreau dissatisfied with poetry's ability to capture the wild? Why does he prefer to look to mythology for expression of the wild?

5   Thoreau believes that the wildest dreams of wild men can hold a truth that sometimes goes beyond common sense. Are Thoreau's examples effective? Explain why you agree or disagree with him.

IDEAS FOR WRITING

1   Write an essay that supports or refutes Thoreau's assertion, "In short, all good things are wild and free."

2   Write an essay, story, or poem about how your life acknowledges and expresses the wild. Be sure to include your definition of "wild" in the piece.

The Etiquette of Freedom

GARY SNYDER

Gary Snyder (b. 1930) grew up in the Pacific Northwest. He earned his B.A. at Reed College and did graduate work at Indiana University and the University of California at Berkeley, where he studied Asian languages, culture, and poetry. Eastern thought and religion have been fundamental to his work since the 1950s. Snyder's poetry explores the relationships between the spiritual and natural worlds. In the 1960s Snyder was involved in many liberal protests, and he continues to write and speak out on peace, environmental awareness, and nuclear weapons. In 1975 he won the Pulitzer Prize in poetry for Turtle Island. *Snyder and his family have been living in the foothills of the Sierra Nevada in northern California for over twenty years. Currently he teaches at the University of California at Davis. Snyder has written sixteen books of poetry and prose. His most recent collections are* The Practice of the Wild *(1990), from which the following selection is excerpted;* No Nature: New and Selected Poems *(1992);* A Place in Space: Ethics, Aesthetics and Watersheds: New and Selected Prose *(1995); and* Mountains and Rivers Without End *(1996).*

Coyote and Ground Squirrel do not break the compact they have with each other that one must play predator and the other play game. In the wild a baby Black-tailed Hare gets maybe one free chance to run across a meadow without looking up. There won't be a second. The sharper the knife, the cleaner the line of the carving. We can appreciate the elegance of the forces that shape life and the world, that have shaped every line of our bodies—teeth and nails, nipples and eyebrows. We also see that we must try to live without causing unnecessary harm, not just to fellow humans but to all beings. We must try not to be stingy, or to exploit others. There will be enough pain in the world as it is. 1

Such are the lessons of the wild. The school where these lessons can be learned, the realms of caribou and elk, elephant and rhinoceros, orca and walrus, are shrinking day by day. Creatures who have traveled with us through the ages are now apparently doomed, as their habitat—and the old, old habitat of humans—falls before the slow-motion explosion of expanding world economies. If the lad or lass is among us who knows where the secret heart of this Growth-Monster is hidden, let them please tell us where to shoot the arrow that will slow it down. And if the secret heart stays secret and our work is made no easier, I for one will keep working for wildness day by day. 2

"Wild and free." An American dream-phrase loosing images: a long-maned stallion racing across the grasslands, a V of Canada Geese high and honking, a squirrel chattering and leaping limb to limb overhead 3 in an oak. It also sounds like an ad for a Harley-Davidson. Both words, profoundly political and sensitive as they are, have become consumer baubles. I hope to investigate the meaning of *wild* and how it connects with *free* and what one would want to do with these meanings. To be truly free one must take on the basic conditions as they are—painful, impermanent, open, imperfect—and then be grateful for impermanence and the freedom it grants us. For in a fixed universe there would be no freedom. With that freedom we improve the campsite, teach children, oust tyrants. The world is nature, and in the long run inevitably wild, because the wild, as the process and essence of nature, is also an ordering of impermanence.

Although *nature* is a term that is not of itself threatening, the idea of   4
the "wild" in civilized societies—both European and Asian—is often associated with unruliness, disorder, and violence. The Chinese word for nature, *zi-ran* (Japanese *shizen*) means "self-thus." It is a bland and general word. The word for wild in Chinese, *ye* (Japanese *ya*), which basically means "open country," has a wide set of meanings: in various combinations the term becomes illicit connection, desert country, an illegitimate child (open-country child), prostitute (open-country flower), and such. In an interesting case, *ye-man zi-yu* ("open-country southern-tribal-person-freedom") means "wild license." In another context "open-country story" becomes "fiction and fictitious romance." Other associations are usually with the rustic and uncouth. In a way *ye* is taken to mean "nature at its worst." Although the Chinese and Japanese have long given lip service to nature, only the early Daoists might have thought that wisdom could come of wildness.

Thoreau says "give me a wildness no civilization can endure."   5
That's clearly not difficult to find. It is harder to imagine a civilization that wildness can endure, yet this is just what we must try to do. Wildness is not just the "preservation of the world," it *is* the world. Civilizations east and west have long been on a collision course with wild nature, and now the developed nations in particular have the witless power to destroy not only individual creatures but whole species, whole processes, of the earth. We need a civilization that can live fully and creatively together with wildness. We must start growing it right here, in the New World.

When we think of wilderness in America today, we think of remote   6
and perhaps designated regions that are commonly alpine, desert, or swamp. Just a few centuries ago, when virtually *all* was wild in North America, wilderness was not something exceptionally severe. Pronghorn and bison trailed through the grasslands, creeks ran full of salmon, there were acres of clams, and grizzlies, cougar, and bighorn sheep were common in the lowlands. There were human beings, too: North America was *all populated*. One might say yes, but thinly— which raises the question of according to whom. The fact is, people were everywhere. When the Spanish foot soldier Alvar Núñez Cabeza de Vaca and his two companions (one of whom was African) were

wrecked on the beach of what is now Galveston, and walked to the Rio Grande valley and then south back into Mexico between 1528 and 1536, there were few times in the whole eight years that they were not staying at a native settlement or camp. They were always on trails.

It has always been part of basic human experience to live in a cul-   7
ture of wilderness. There has been no wilderness without some kind of human presence for several hundred thousand years. Nature is not a place to visit, it is *home*—and within that home territory there are more familiar and less familiar places. Often there are areas that are difficult and remote, but all are *known* and even named. One August I was at a pass in the Brooks Range of northern Alaska at the head-waters of the Koyukuk River, a green three-thousand-foot tundra pass between the broad ranges, open and gentle, dividing the waters that flow to the Arctic Sea from the Yukon. It is as remote a place as you could be in North America, no roads, and the trails are those made by migrating caribou. Yet this pass has been steadily used by Inupiaq people of the north slope and Athapaskan people of the Yukon as a regular north-south trade route for at least seven thousand years.

All of the hills and lakes of Alaska have been named in one or an-   8
other of the dozen or so languages spoken by the native people, as the researchers of Jim Kari and others have shown. Euro-American map-makers name these places after transient exploiters, or their own girl-friends, or home towns in the Lower 48. The point is: it's all in the native story, yet only the tiniest trace of human presence through all that time shows. The place-based stories the people tell, and the nam-ing they've done, is their archaeology, architecture, and *title* to the land. Talk about living lightly.

Cultures of wilderness live by the life and death lessons of sub-   9
sistence economies. But what can we now mean by the words *wild* and for that matter *nature*? Languages meander like great rivers leav-ing oxbow traces over forgotten beds, to be seen only from the air or by scholars. Language is like some kind of infinitely interfertile family of species spreading or mysteriously declining over time, shamelessly and endlessly hybridizing, changing its own rules as it goes. Words are used as signs, as stand-ins, arbitrary and temporary, even as language reflects (and informs) the shifting values of the peoples whose minds it inhabits and glides through. We have faith in "meaning" the way we might believe in wolverines—putting trust in the occasional reports of others or on the authority of once seeing a pelt. But it is sometimes worth tracking these tricksters back.

The Words Nature, Wild, *and* Wilderness

Take *nature* first. The word *nature is* from Latin *natura*, "birth, con-   10
stitution, character, course of things"—ultimately from *nasci*, to be born. So we have *nation, natal, native, pregnant*. The probable Indo-

European root (via Greek *gna*—hence cognate, agnate) is *gen* (Sanskrit *jan*), which provides *generate* and *genus*, as well as *kin* and *kind*.

The word gets two slightly different meanings. One is "the out-   11
doors"—the physical world, including all living things. Nature by this definition is a norm of the world that is apart from the features or products of civilization and human will. The machine, the artifact, the devised, or the extraordinary (like a two-headed calf) is spoken of as "unnatural." The other meaning, which is broader, is "the material world or its collective objects and phenomena," including the products of human action and intention. As an agency nature is defined as "the creative and regulative physical power which is conceived of as operating in the material world and as the immediate cause of all its phenomena." Science and some sorts of mysticism rightly propose that *everything* is natural. By these lights there is nothing unnatural about New York City, or toxic wastes, or atomic energy, and nothing— by definition—that we do or experience in life is "unnatural."

(The "supernatural"? One way to deal with it is to say that "the super-   12
natural" is a name for phenomena which are reported by so few people as to leave their reality in doubt. Nonetheless these events—ghosts, gods, magical transformations, and such—are described often enough to make them continue to be intriguing and, for some, credible.)

The physical universe and all its properties—I would prefer to use   13
the word *nature* in this sense. But it will come up meaning "The out- doors" or "other-than-human" sometimes even here.

The word *wild* is like a gray fox trotting off through the forest, duck-   14
ing behind bushes, going in and out of sight. Up close, first glance, it is "wild"—then farther into the woods next glance it's "wyld" and it recedes via Old Norse *villr* and Old Teutonic *wilthijaz* into a faint pre-Teutonic *ghweltijos* which means, still, wild and maybe wooded (*wald*) and lurks back there with possible connections to *will*, to Latin *silva* (forest, sauvage), and to the Indo-European root *ghwer,* base of Latin *ferus* (feral, fierce), which swings us around to Thoreau's "awful ferity" shared by virtuous people and lovers. The Oxford English Dictionary has it this way:

> Of animals—not tame, undomesticated, unruly.
>
> Of plants—not cultivated.
>
> Of land—uninhabited, uncultivated.
>
> Of foodcrops—produced or yielded without cultivation.
>
> Of societies—uncivilized, rude, resisting constituted government.
>
> Of individuals—unrestrained, insubordinate, licentious, dissolute, loose. "Wild and wanton widowes"—1614.
>
> Of behavior—violent, destructive, cruel, unruly.
>
> Of behavior—artless, free, spontaneous. "Warble his native woodnotes wild"—John Milton.

Wild is largely defined in our dictionaries by what—from a human   15
standpoint—it is not. It cannot be seen by this approach for what it *is*.
Turn it the other way:

> Of animals—free agents, each with its own endowments, living
> within natural systems.
>
> Of plants—self-propagating, self-maintaining, flourishing in
> accord with innate qualities.
>
> Of land—a place where the original and potential vegetation and
> fauna are intact and in full interaction and the landforms are
> entirely the result of nonhuman forces. Pristine.
>
> Of foodcrops—food supplies made available and sustainable by
> the natural excess and exuberance of wild plants in their growth
> and in the production of quantities of fruit or seeds.
>
> Of societies—societies whose order has grown from within and is
> maintained by the force of consensus and custom rather than ex-
> plicit legislation. Primary cultures, which consider themselves the
> original and eternal inhabitants of their territory. Societies which
> resist economic and political domination by civilization. Societies
> whose economic system is in a close and sustainable relation to
> the local ecosystem.
>
> Of individuals—following local custom, style, and etiquette with-
> out concern for the standards of the metropolis or nearest trading
> post. Unintimidated, self-reliant, independent. "Proud and free."
>
> Of behavior—fiercely resisting any oppression, confinement, or
> exploitation. Far-out, outrageous, "bad," admirable.
>
> Of behavior—artless, free, spontaneous, unconditioned. Expres-
> sive, physical, openly sexual, ecstatic.

Most of the senses in this second set of definitions come very close   16
to being how the Chinese define the term *Dao*, the *way* of Great Nature:
eluding analysis, beyond categories, self-organizing, self-informing,
playful, surprising, impermanent, insubstantial, independent, complete, orderly, unmediated, freely manifesting, self-authenticating, self-
willed, complex, quite simple. Both empty and real at the same time. In
some cases we might call it sacred. It is not far from the Buddhist term
Dharma with its original senses of forming and firming.

The word *wilderness*, earlier *wyldernesse*, Old English *wildeornes*,   17
possibly from "wild-deer-ness" (*deor*, deer and other forest animals)
but more likely "wildern-ness," has the meanings:

> A large area of wild land, with original vegetation and wildlife,
> ranging from dense jungle or rainforest to arctic or alpine "white
> wilderness."
>
> A wasteland, as an area unused or useless for agriculture or pasture.

A space of sea or air, as in Shakespeare, "I stand as one upon a Rock, environ'd with a Wilderness of Sea" (*Titus Andronicus*). The oceans.

A place of danger and difficulty: where you take your own chances, depend on your own skills, and do not count on rescue.

This world as contrasted with heaven. "I walked through the wildernesse of this world" (*Pilgrim's Progress*).

A place of abundance, as in John Milton, "a wildernesse of sweets."

Milton's usage of wilderness catches the very real condition of energy and richness that is so often found in wild systems. "A wildernesse of sweets" is like the billions of herring or mackerel babies in the ocean, the cubic miles of krill, wild prairie grass seed (leading to the bread of this day, made from the germs of grasses)—all the incredible fecundity of small animals and plants, feeding the web. But from another side, wilderness has implied chaos, eros, the unknown, realms of taboo, the habitat of both the ecstatic and the demonic. In both senses it is a place of archetypal power, teaching, and challenge. 18

QUESTIONS FOR DISCUSSION

1 Where does Snyder most clearly state his purpose in writing this essay?

2 According to Snyder, in what ways are the concepts of the wild and freedom similar? How are they connected?

3 Why does Snyder study the meaning of words? How does he believe that words and languages grow?

4 Why does Snyder present various meanings of the words *nature* and *wild*? What did you learn about these concepts from his information?

5 Snyder believes that we need to nurture a wilderness in our country. Explain why you agree or disagree with him.

IDEAS FOR WRITING

1 Develop an essay that shows how the thinking of Henry David Thoreau, Ralph Waldo Emerson, and Aldo Leopold about the wilderness and the wild may have influenced Snyder.

2 If you agree with Snyder that we need to nurture the wilderness areas in our country, write a paper that presents what has already been done and what still needs to be done to preserve wilderness areas; if you disagree, write an essay that is critical of Snyder's point of view.

She Unnames Them

URSULA K. LE GUIN

*The daughter of an anthropologist and a writer, Ursula Le Guin
(b. 1929) grew up in Berkeley, California, earned her B.A. at Radcliffe
College in 1951, and did graduate work at Columbia University.
Le Guin has published more than eighty short stories, sixteen novels,
ten books for children, several volumes of poetry, and two collections
of essays. She has won many distinguished awards, including the
Nebula and Hugo awards for science fiction and the National Book
Award. Some of her best-known novels are* The Left Hand of Darkness
(1969), The Lathe of Heaven *(1971),* The Dispossessed *(1974), and*
The Earthsea Trilogy *(1977). In 1993 she edited the* Norton Book of
Science Fiction. *Recently she published the collection* Unlocking the
Air and Other Stories *(1996). Speaking of the process of creating her
fiction, Le Guin says, "It seems to me that most of an artist's job is to
be ready, to have the skills perfected. . . . You're just wandering around
the wave lengths and something comes through." The selection that
follows is included in* Dancing at the Edge of the World *(1990), a
collection of stories and essays.*

Most of them accepted namelessness with the perfect indifference   1
with which they had so long accepted and ignored their names.
Whales and dolphins, seals and sea otters consented with particular
grace and alacrity, sliding into anonymity as into their element. A faction of yaks, however, protested. They said that "yak" sounded right,
and that almost everyone who knew they existed called them that.
Unlike the ubiquitous creatures such as rats and fleas, who had been
called by hundreds or thousands of different names since Babel, the
yaks could truly say, they said, that they had a *name*. They discussed
the matter all summer. The councils of the elderly females finally
agreed that though the name might be useful to others it was so re-
dundant from the yak point of view that they never spoke it themselves and hence might as well dispense with it. After they presented
the argument in this light to their bulls, a full consensus was delayed
only by the onset of severe early blizzards. Soon after the beginning of
the thaw, their agreement was reached and the designation "yak" was
returned to the donor.

Among the domestic animals, few horses had cared what anybody   2
called them since the failure of Dean Swift's attempt to name them
from their own vocabulary. Cattle, sheep, swine, asses, mules, and
goats, along with chickens, geese, and turkeys, all agreed enthusiasti-
cally to give their names back to the people to whom—as they put it—
they belonged.

A couple of problems did come up with pets. The cats, of course, 3
steadfastly denied ever having had any name other than those self-
given, unspoken, ineffably personal names which, as the poet named
Eliot said, they spend long hours daily contemplating—though none
of the contemplators has ever admitted that what they contemplate is
their names and some onlookers have wondered if the object of the
meditative gaze might not in fact be the Perfect, or Platonic, Mouse. In
any case, it is a moot point now. It was with the dogs, and with some
parrots, lovebirds, ravens, and mynahs, that the trouble arose. These
verbally talented individuals insisted that their names were important
to them, and flatly refused to part with them. But as soon as they
understood that the issue was precisely one of individual choice, and
that anybody who wanted to be called Rover, or Froufrou, or Polly, or
even Birdie in the personal sense, was perfectly free to do so, not one
of them had the least objection to parting with the lowercase (or, as re-
gards German creatures, uppercase) generic appellations "poodle,"
"parrot," "dog," or "bird," and all the Linnaean qualifiers that had trailed
along behind them for two hundred years like tin cans tied to a tail.

The insects parted with their names in vast clouds and swarms of 4
ephemeral syllables buzzing and stinging and humming and flitting
and crawling and tunnelling away.

As for the fish of the sea, their names dispersed from them in si- 5
lence throughout the oceans like faint, dark blurs of cuttlefish ink, and
drifted off on the currents without a trace.

None were left now to unname, and yet how close I felt to them 6
when I saw one of them swim or fly or trot or crawl across my way or
over my skin, or stalk me in the night, or go along beside me for a
while in the day. They seemed far closer than when their names had
stood between myself and them like a clear barrier: so close that my
fear of them and their fear of me became one same fear. And the attraction that many of us felt, the desire to smell one another's smells,
feel or rub or caress one another's scales or skin or feathers or fur, taste
one another's blood or flesh, keep one another warm—that attraction
was now all one with the fear, and the hunter could not be told from
the hunted, nor the eater from the food.

This was more or less the effect I had been after. It was somewhat 7
more powerful than I had anticipated, but I could not now, in all conscience, make an exception for myself. I resolutely put anxiety away,
went to Adam, and said, "You and your father lent me this—gave it to
me, actually. It's been really useful, but it doesn't exactly seem to fit
very well lately. But thanks very much! It's really been very useful."

It is hard to give back a gift without sounding peevish or ungrate- 8
ful, and I did not want to leave him with that impression of me. He
was not paying much attention, as it happened, and said only, "Put it
down over there, O.K.?" and went on with what he was doing.

One of my reasons for doing what I did was that talk was getting us   9
nowhere, but all the same I felt a little let down. I had been prepared
to defend my decision. And I thought that perhaps when he did notice he might be upset and want to talk. I put some things away and
fiddled around a little, but he continued to do what he was doing and
to take no notice of anything else. At last I said, "Well, goodbye, dear.
I hope the garden key turns up."

He was fitting parts together, and said, without looking around,   10
"O.K., fine, dear. When's dinner?"

"I'm not sure," I said. "I'm going now. With the—" I hesitated, and   11
finally said, "With them, you know," and went on out. In fact, I had
only just then realized how hard it would have been to explain myself.
I could not chatter away as I used to do, taking it all for granted. My
words now must be as slow, as new, as single, as tentative as the steps
I took going down the path away from the house, between the dark-
branched, tall dancers motionless against the winter shining.

QUESTIONS FOR DISCUSSION

1   According to the narrator, why do most animals accept namelessness with "perfect indifference"? What animals resisted giving
up their names, and why? What does this suggest about the cus-
tom of naming animals and other living things?

2   How does Le Guin use the sounds of language, including words
that sound like what they are describing, to emphasize her "revi-
sioning" of the relations of humans to the animal kingdom? Can
you think of any animals that resemble the names people have
given them?

3   How do the relationships between the narrator and the creatures
of the earth, air, and water change after the unnaming? What
does this imply about the barriers that names create between
people and animals?

4   What is the significance of the narrator's conversation with Adam
and her parting remarks to him? Why does Adam fail to respond
to her decision to "give back" her name?

5   If the narrator is Eve, and if she has decided to leave Adam, where
will she go? What does the last phrase of the story suggest about
her new sense of language and awareness of nature?

IDEAS FOR WRITING

1   Write an essay that explains the story's meaning. Do you agree
with Le Guin's perspective on the state of the world and the role
of language?

2   Write a sequel to this story. Describe the narrator's new world.

Sea Change

KATHLEEN NORRIS

Kathleen Norris (b. 1947) was born in Washington, D.C., and raised in Hawaii. She graduated from Bennington College in Vermont with a B.A. in 1969. After living in New York City for several years, she inherited her family's ranch corporation when her father died. Norris moved back to South Dakota with her husband, where she began her career as a writer and the manager of the ranch corporation. Although she is officially a Presbyterian, for the past ten years Norris has been an oblate of Assumption Abbey, a Benedictine monastery in North Dakota. The Great Plains and her religious life have been the inspiration for much of her writing. Several of Norris's most widely read poetry collections are Poetry: Falling Off *(1971),* The Middle of the World *(1981), and* Little Girls in Church *(1995). Her nonfiction—* Dakota: A Spiritual Geography *(1993),* The Cloister Walk *(1996), and* Amazing Grace: A Vocabulary of Faith *(1998)—speaks of life in the Great Plains to emphasize spiritual values while offering alternative ways of understanding time and place. In "Sea Change," included in* Dakota, *Norris encourages her readers to imagine, combat, and embrace the challenges of life on the Great Plains with its great expanse of land.*

> Calenture: a disease incident to sailors within the tropics, characterized by delirium in which the patient, it is said, fancies the sea to be green fields and desires to leap into it.
>
> —OXFORD ENGLISH DICTIONARY

> The atmosphere of the sea persists in Perkins County.
>
> —DAVID J. HOLDEN, *DAKOTA VISIONS*

My move from New York City to western South Dakota changed my sense of time and space so radically I might as well have gone to sea. In journeying on the inland ocean of the Plains, the great void at the heart of North America, I've discovered that time and distance, those inconveniences that modern life with its increasingly sophisticated computer technologies seeks to erase, have a reality and a terrifying beauty all their own.

Like all who choose life in the slow lane—sailors, monks, farmers—I partake of a contemplative reality. Living close to such an expanse of land I find I have little incentive to move fast, little need of instant information. I have learned to trust the processes that take time, to value change that is not sudden or ill-considered but grows out of the ground of experience. Such change is properly defined as conversion, a word that at its root connotes not a change of essence but of perspective, as turning round; turning back to or returning; turning one's attention to.

Both monasteries and the rural communities on the Plains are   3
places where nothing much happens. Paradoxically, they are also places where being open to conversion is most necessary if community is to survive. The inner impulse toward conversion, a change of heart, may be muted in a city, where outward change is fast, noisy, ever-present. But in the small town, in the quiet arena, a refusal to grow (which is one way Gregory of Nyssa defined sin) makes any constructive change impossible. Both monasteries and small towns lose their ability to be truly hospitable to the stranger when people use them as a place to hide out, a place to escape from the demands of life.

Because of the monotony of the monastic life, the bad thought of   4
boredom (or acedia, the noonday demon) has traditionally been thought to apply particularly to monks, but I think most people have endured a day or two along the lines of this fourth-century description by the monk Evagrius:

> It makes it seem that the sun barely moves, if at all, and the day is fifty hours long. Then it constrains the monk to look constantly out the window, to walk outside the cell to gaze carefully at the sun and determine how far it stands from the dinner hour, to look now this way and that to see if perhaps one of the brethren appears from his cell.

Anyone living in isolated or deprived circumstances, whether in a   5
monastery or a quiet little town on the Great Plains, is susceptible to the noonday demon. It may appear as an innocuous question; "Isn't the mail here yet?" But, as monks have always known, such restlessness can lead to profound despair that makes a person despise his or her neighbors, work, and even life itself. Perhaps the noonday demon helps explain the high rate of alcoholism found in underpopulated steppes, whether in Siberia or the American West.

Ever since moving to western Dakota, I've wondered if the version   6
of the demon we experience here isn't a kind of calenture, a prairie version of the sea fever that afflicted sailors several centuries ago. The vast stretch of undulating land before us can make us forget ourselves, make us do foolish things.

I almost think that to be a good citizen of the Plains one must   7
choose the life consciously, as one chooses the monastery. One must make an informed rejection of any other way of life and also undergo a period of formation. Some of the ranch families I know in Dakota are raising their children in the way Benedict asks monasteries to treat would-be monks, warning, "Do not grant newcomers to the monastic life an easy entry."

These parents do not encourage their children to take up the hard   8
and economically uncertain life of farming and ranching. Instead,

they provide them with the opportunity to see what is available in other careers, in other places. And most of the young people move on. But, as one couple recently told me of their daughter, "She's traveled, she's seen the outside world. And it's not that she's afraid of it or couldn't live there, she's decided she doesn't need it. She wants to come back here."

They're hoping she will find a teaching job in the area, not a great   9 prospect in the current economic environment, when many Dakota schools are consolidating or closing. But what interests me about her parents' remark is how like monastic formation directors they sound. They, too, want people who have lived a little, who have seen the world, and, in the words of one monk, "know exactly what it is they're giving up." He added, "The hard part is that this has to become all they need. The monastery has to become their home."

Making the Plains a home means accepting its limitations and not,   10 as so many townspeople do even in drought years, watering a lawn to country club perfection. Making this all we need means accepting that we are living in the arid plains of western South Dakota, not in Connecticut (which has the rainfall to sustain such greenery) or Palm Springs (which doesn't but has the money to pretend otherwise). Once the water runs out, the money won't be worth much.

I wonder if the calentures don't explain why, from the first days of   11 white settlement, Dakotans of the West River have tried to recreate the land before them in the image of the rain-blessed places they knew, the rich farmland back East in New York or Virginia, or the old country farmland of Sweden, or Scotland. Encouraged by the railroads and the government to pretend that the land could support families on homestead allotments of 160 acres, they believed the rural economy could maintain small towns nine or ten miles apart, the distance a steam locomotive could go before needing more water. But, in trying to make this place like the places they had known, they would not allow it to be itself.

Eastern North and South Dakota have enough rainfall and popula-   12 tion density to hang on at the western fringes of the Midwest, having more in common with Minnesota and Iowa than with Montana. But in western Dakota, the harsh climate and the vast expanse of the land have forced people, through a painful process of attrition, to adjust to this country on its own terms and live accordingly: ranches of several thousand acres, towns that serve as economic centers forty or sixty miles apart. Taking the slow boat to Dakota, driving in from the East, the reality of the land asserts itself and you begin to understand how the dreams of early settlers were worn away.

Heading west out of Minneapolis on Highway 12, you pass through   13 150 miles of rich Minnesota farmland, through towns that look like New England villages with tall trees well over a hundred years old. These are sizeable towns by Dakota standards: Litchfield (pop. 5,900),

Willmar (15,900), Benson (3,600). South Dakota is visible, a high ridge on the horizon, long before the crossing a few miles past Ortonville (pop. 2,550, elev. 1,094).

Your first town in South Dakota is Big Stone City (pop. 630, elev. 977) 14 at the southern edge of Big Stone Lake, named for huge granite out-croppings in the area. Here you begin your climb from the broad Min-nesota River Valley to what French trappers termed the "Coteaux des Prairies" or prairie hills of eastern South Dakota. This is the beginning of the drift prairie of eastern North and South Dakota, named for the glacial deposits, or drift, that make up its topsoil. The road narrows, twisting around small hills and shallow coulees. You pass by several small, spring-fed lakes formed by glaciers and several good-size towns: Milbank (pop. 3,800), Webster (2,000), Groton (1,100).

After Groton you cross the James River Valley, its soil rich with 15 glacial loam deposits. By the time you reach the city of Aberdeen, South Dakota (pop. 25,000, elev. 1,304), one hundred miles from the Minnesota border, you are in open farm country with more of a gentle roll to it than eastern Kansas, but basically flat and treeless except for shelterbelts around farmhouses and trees planted and carefully tended in the towns.

Driving west from Aberdeen you find that the towns are fewer and 16 smaller, with more distance between them: Ipswich (pop. 965), Roscoe (362), Bowdle (590), Selby (707). One hundred miles west of Aberdeen you come to Mobridge (pop. 3,768, elev. 1,676), on the banks of the Missouri River.

What John Steinbeck said in *Travels with Charley* about the Mis- 17 souri River crossing 120 miles to the north is true of the Mobridge crossing as well. He wrote: "Here's the boundary between east and west. On the Bismarck side it is eastern landscape, eastern grass, with the look and smell of eastern America. Across the Missouri on the Mandan side it is pure west with brown grass and water scorings and small outcrops. The two sides of the river might well be a thousand miles apart."

The boundary is an ancient one. The deep gorge of the Missouri 18 marks the western edge of the Wisconsin ice sheet that once covered most of north central America. Passing through Mobridge and cross-ing the river you take a steep climb through rugged hills onto the high plateau that extends west all the way to the Rockies. Lewis and Clark marked this border by noting that the tallgrass to the east (bluestem, switch grass, Indian grass) grew six to eight feet high, while the short-grass in the west (needle-and-thread, western wheat grass, blue grama grass, and upland sedges) topped at about four feet. You have left the glacial drift prairie for a land whose soil is the residue of prehistoric seas that have come and gone, weathered shale and limestone that is far less fertile than the land to the east but good for grazing sheep and cattle. Here you set your watch to Mountain time.

Here, also, you may have to combat disorientation and an over-   19
whelming sense of loneliness. Plunged into the pale expanse of short-
grass country, you either get your sea legs or want to bail out. As the
road twists and turns through open but hilly country, climbing 325
feet in twenty-two miles to the town of McLaughlin (pop. 780), you
begin to realize you have left civilization behind. You are on the high
plains, where there are almost no trees, let alone other people. You
find that the towns reassuringly listed every ten miles or so on your
map (Walker, McIntosh, Watauga, Morristown, Keldron, Thunder
Hawk) offer very little in the way of services. All but McIntosh (pop.
300) have populations well under a hundred. You climb imperceptibly
through rolling hayfields and pasture land punctuated by wheat or
sunflower fields for another eighty miles or so before you reach another town of any size—Lemmon (pop. 1,616, elev. 2,577).

You should have filled your gas tank in Aberdeen, especially if   20
you're planning to travel after dark. For many years there was no gaso-
line available at night (except in the summer) between Aberdeen and
Miles City, Montana, a distance of nearly four hundred miles. Currently there are two 24-hour stations in towns nearly 200 miles apart.
On the last stretch, the 78 miles from Baker, Montana, to Miles City,
there are no towns at all, just a spectacularly desolate moonspace
of sagebrush. Farmers will usually give or sell a little gas to stranded
travelers, and small-town police forces often have keys to the local
service stations so they can sell you enough to get you on your way.
But the message is clear: you're in the West now. Pay attention to your
gas gauge. Pay attention, period.

But it's hard to pay attention when there is so much nothing to take   21
in, so much open land that evokes in many people a panicked desire to
get through it as quickly as possible. A writer whose name I have forgotten once remarked, "Driving through eastern Montana is like waiting for Godot." I know this only because a Lemmon Public Library
patron brought me the quote, wanting to know who or what Godot
was. It struck me that the writer may as well have been talking about
the landscape of Dakota from Mobridge or Mandan west. And it
seemed appropriate that the good citizen of the region wanted to know
if her homeland was being praised or put down. Had he lived here, I
wonder if Beckett would have found it necessary to write the play.

But people do live here, and many of them will tell you in all hon-   22
esty that they wouldn't live anyplace else. Monks often say the same
thing about their monasteries, and get the same looks of incompre-
hension. People who can't imagine not having more stimulation in
their lives will ask, "How can you do it?" or, "Why do it?" If those questions are answerable for either a monk or a Plains resident, they can't
be answered in a few quick words but in the slow example of a lifetime. The questioner must take the process of endless waiting into
account, as well as the pull of the sea change, of conversion.

Often, when I'm sitting in a monastery choir stall, I wonder how I 23
got there. I could trace it back, as I can trace the route from back East
to western South Dakota. But I'm having too much fun. The words of
Psalms, spoken aloud and left to resonate in the air around me, push
me into new time and space. I think of it as the quantum effect: here
time flows back and forth, in and out of both past and future, and I,
too, am changed.

Being continually open to change, to conversion, is a Benedictine 24
ideal: in fact, it's a vow unique to those who follow Benedict's *Rule*.
This might seem like a paradox, as monks, life farmers, stay in one
place and have a daily routine that can seem monotonous even to
them. But the words spark like a welder's flame; they keep flowing, like
a current carrying me farther than I had intended to go. At noon
prayer we hear the scripture about "sharing the lot of the saints in
light," and in the afternoon I read in a book about quantum physics
that some scientists believe that one day everything will exist in the
form of light. At vespers the text is from I John: "Beloved, we are God's
children now; what we will be has not yet been revealed."

The sun is setting and a nearly full, fat-faced moon is rising above 25
the prairie. We have time on our hands here, in our hearts, and it
makes us strange. I barely passed elementary algebra, but somehow
the vast space before me makes perfectly comprehensible the words
of a mathematician I encountered today: it is easy to "demonstrate
that there are no more minutes in all of eternity than there are in say,
one minute."

The vespers hymn reads: "May God ever dress our days / in peace 26
and starlight order," and I think of old Father Stanley, who said not
long before he died: "I wish to see the Alpha and the Omega." He'd
been a monk for over fifty years, a Dakotan for more than eighty.
It's a dangerous place, this vast ocean of prairie. Something happens
to us here.

QUESTIONS FOR DISCUSSION

1   How does Norris define and develop the contrasts between the
    concepts of conversion and change? Why does she experience
    time and herself from another perspective in the South Dakota
    Plains?

2   In what ways are the concepts of noonday demon, calenture, and
    sea fever similar? Present an example that illustrates your under-
    standing of this state of mind/being.

3   How does Norris describe and explain the ancient boundary be-
    tween East and West in the United States? What does the bound-
    ary symbolize?

4   Why is "Sea Change" an appropriate title for this essay? Discuss how the title embodies several of Norris's major themes in the essay.

5   Interpret Norris's final claim about the Plains and monastic life: "It's a dangerous place, this vast ocean of prairie. Something happens to us here."

IDEAS FOR WRITING

1   Write an essay that explains and expresses your understanding of "sea change" as it is presented in Norris's essay. In developing your ideas, refer to experiences that you have had in natural places, or poems and stories that you have read, that help you to understand Norris's concept. Refer to specific lines in the essay as you build your point of view.

2   Start with Norris and then refer to other writers in this anthology to develop an essay that reflects on the meanings of open space. You can also include your own experiences to clarify your understanding of open space and its impact on the mind and the spirit.

> **CONNECTONS: TOPICS FOR THOUGHT,
> RESEARCH, AND WRITING**

1   Write an extended definition of the word *nature*. In shaping your definition, refer to a dictionary or an encyclopedia, relevant selections in this anthology, and your personal experiences.

2   Write an essay that explores a social, political, or environmental issue that is related to the conflicts created by those who value scientific progress and those who value nature—for example, genetic engineering, artificial intelligence, or surrogate motherhood.

3   Research an environmental issue that affects the quality of life in your community. Write a paper that presents your point of view on this issue. You might also submit your paper to a community or campus newspaper.

4   Write an essay that presents your point of view about the relationships between nature and human behavior. Refer to thinkers such as Emerson, Thoreau, or Gould, as well as to your own personal experiences, to support your theory.

5   Write an essay or story about an intense, challenging experience that you have had in nature. What did you learn about the natural world and yourself through your experience?

6   Write an essay that presents your point of view on the best way to understand nature. You might consider why you rely on scientific knowledge, intuition, experience, culture.

7   Write an essay that explores your thoughts and feelings about the spiritual and thought-provoking power of nature. Refer to writers in this anthology and your own experiences as you develop your response.

8   Participate in an environmental project in your community. Then write an essay for your classmates that explains the project—its purpose and goals—and reflects on what you learned through your participation in the event.

9   Do research into a cultural or religious community that values nature for reasons that are different from those in your culture. Write a comparison and contrast paper that discusses and reflects on what you have learned.

10   Watch one of the following films (or one of your own choice that explores an issue related to nature and the environment):

Zabriskie Point (1970)

Walkabout—Restored Director's Cut (1970)

The Last Wave (1977)

Whale for the Killing (1981)

Never Cry Wolf (1983)

The River (1984)
Out of Africa (1985)
The Emerald Forest (1985)
Gorillas in the Mist (1988)
Mind Walk (1991)
The Milagro Beanfield War (1993)

Then write a paper that explains how the film's themes comment on our relationship and responsibility to the natural world.

Acknowledgments

Rachel Carson, "The Obligation to Endure," from *Silent Spring*. Copyright © 1962 by Rachel L. Carson, renewed 1990 by Roger Christie. Reprinted by permission of Houghton Mifflin Company. All rights reserved.

Lorna Dee Cervantes, "Emplumada," from *Emplumada*. Copyright © 1981 by Lorna Dee Cervantes. Reprinted by permission of the University of Pittsburgh Press.

Annie Dillard, "Total Eclipse," from *Teaching a Stone to Talk*. Copyright © 1982 by Annie Dillard. Reprinted by permission of HarperCollins Publishers, Inc.

Gretel Ehrlich, "The Solace of Open Spaces," from *The Solace of Open Spaces*. Copyright © 1985 by Gretel Ehrlich. Used by permission of Viking Penguin, a division of Penguin Putnam, Inc.

Dian Fossey, excerpt from *Gorillas in the Mist*. Copyright © 1983 by Dian Fossey. Reprinted by permission of Houghton Mifflin Company. All rights reserved.

Stephen Jay Gould, "Evolution as Fact and Theory." Copyright © 1981 by Stephen Jay Gould. Reprinted by permission of the author.

Jon Krakauer, excerpt from *Into Thin Air*. Copyright © 1997 by Jon Krakauer. Reprinted by permission of Villard Books, a division of Random House, Inc.

Ursula K. Le Guin, "She Unnames Them," from *Buffalo Gals and Other Animal Presences*. Copyright © 1985 by Ursula K. Le Guin. First appeared in *The New Yorker*. Reprinted by permission of the author and the author's agent, the Virginia Kidd Agency, Inc.

Aldo Leopold, "Thinking Like a Mountain," from *A Sand County Almanac: With Other Essays on Conservation from Round River*. Copyright © 1949, 1953, 1966, renewed 1977, 1981 by Oxford University Press, Inc. Used by permission of Oxford University Press, Inc.

Barry Holstun Lopez, "The Stone Horse," from *Crossing Open Ground*, Scribner's & Sons. Reprinted by permission of Sterling Lord Literistic, Inc. Copyright © 1988 by Barry Holstun Lopez.

Farley Mowat, excerpt from *Never Cry Wolf*. Copyright © 1963 by Farley Mowat, Limited. Reprinted by permission of Little Brown and Company. Also used by permission of the Canadian publishers, McClelland & Stewart, Inc.

Kathleen Norris, "Sea Change," from *Dakota*. Copyright © 1993 by Kathleen Norris. Reprinted by permission of Ticknor & Fields/Houghton Mifflin Company. All rights reserved.